TRIUMPH

SOY-FREE VEGAN WHOLEFOODS FOR ALL APPETITES

HILDA JORGENSEN

Introduction

About the Recipe Symbols

GF Gluten-Free. These recipes contain no gluten or oats.

NSI No Specialty Ingredients. All the ingredients needed for these recipes can be found in a typical supermarket.

LF Low fat. These recipes contain less than 1 teaspoon of fat per serve.

NF Nightshade-Free. These recipes do not contain any potatoes, tomatoes, capiscums, chillis or eggplants.

OGF Onion- and Garlic-Free. These recipes contain no ingredients from the onion and garlic family of vegetables.

(Under 45 minutes) Under 45 minutes. These recipes take less than 45 minutes in total, including preparation time.

When cooking for people with allergies be sure to check the ingredients list of any pre-made products used, such as vegan milk, tomato ketchup and baking powder, to ensure they are suitable.

About the Recipes

The recipes in this book have been designed to satisfy hunger and nutritional needs, while still tasting great. Pages 8 and 9 detail some of the nutritional considerations that vegans need to make, and the first of these is protein. Chapters 2, 3, 4 and 6 contain protein-rich dishes which form the centre of the meal. Sometimes they also have plenty of carbohydrates to satisfy immediate hunger, and all they require is a simple garden salad to form a complete meal. For other recipes it's a good idea to serve them with a cooked wholegrain (page 12), or one of the potato side dishes from chapter 7, and these recipes have been photographed with the grain or side-dish, to show what the completed meal looks like.

Chapters 8-10 are sweet dishes made without any refined flours, margarine, or egg replacer. These dishes prove that there is no need to sacrifice taste or texture in a dessert in order to eat a vegan wholefoods diet.

I hope that these recipes will inspire you to appreciate and rely on your own healthy vegan home cooking. If you have any questions or feedback, please feel free to contact me through my website: http://triumphofthelentil.wordpress.com

Replacing Soy

TVP or TSP (textured vegetable protein) To replace this, use a mixture of barley (or brown rice for gluten-free) and brown lentils, the same amount dry as is called for of dry TVP. Instead of soaking the TVP, cook the lentils and barley for half an hour, or until tender but not mushy. The lentils add protein while the barley adds a chewy texture. You will see this being used in my shepherds pie, moussaka and party pie recipes.

Soy flour Replace 1 for 1 with chickpea flour

Silken tofu is a tricky one, it depends on what it is being used for. Sometimes it is used as an egg replacer, in which it can be replaced by an appropriate mix from the egg replacing section on page 7. Sometimes it is used for creamy sauces, in this case a blended mixture of half cashews and half water will work.

Mashed tofu in loaves and burgers can be replaced by mashed vegetables or beans, with some chickpea flour added.

Replacing Soy, continued

Soy sauce and tamari can be replaced with vegan worcestershire sauce, coconut aminos or soy-free tamari. If it's not a dominant flavour in a dish, then adding extra salt will also work. Adding fresh mushrooms to the dish will also work in some cases, or using the liquid from soaking dried mushrooms. Some worchestershire sauces contain soy, so be sure to check the ingredients.

Sneaky Soy

Soy manages to sneak itself into quite a few foods. It is often labeled as 'emulsifier' in many things including chocolate, frozen pastry and vegan ice cream, to name a few. Some people with soy allergies can tolerate a little bit of this emulsifier (soya lecithin, 476 and 322) while others can't. There are many kinds of vegan chocolate around that don't contain this emulsifier, so be sure to check the ingredients if you want your food to be completely free of soy. 'Vegetable oil' can be a sneaky name for soybean oil, found in some processed foods, although 'vegetable oil' is not always soy, and is typically palm oil. Some organic sauces, baked beans and other products will contain tamari in the ingredients so it's worth checking those as well. While tamari can be made without soy, most of the stuff out there is soy-based, the same applies to miso.

Replacing Eggs

I generally use a mixture of chickpea flour and water to replace eggs. This is easy, as it usually just involves adding the flour to the dry ingredients, and water to the wet mixture. It adds extra protein, and is also very reliable and realistic. To use this as an egg replacer in someone else's recipe, use 1/4 cup chickpea flour and 1/4 cup water for every egg. Chickpea flour is a flour made from whole raw chickpeas, can be found in health food shops, along with Indian, French and Italian grocers. It is also known as besan, chana flour, gram flour, cici flour and garbanzo bean flour.

Ground flaxseeds (linseeds) and whole chia seeds are also good egg replacers, adding extra nutrition along with their binding properties. To replace an egg using one of these, mix 1 heaped tablespoon of ground flaxseeds or whole chia seeds with 1/4 cup of boiling water and leave this to sit for a minute or so, until it thickens. To replace chickpea flour with one of these in my recipes, reduce the liquid in the recipe by 1/4 cup for every 1/4 cup of chickpea flour called for, and add this liquid instead as boiling water to the seed meal.

Mashed bananas and fruit purées such as apple sauce also work as egg replacers in sweet dishes, use 1/4 cup of these for every egg called for in a recipe; or to use these in my recipes, replace every 1/4 cup of chickpea flour and 1/4 cup of water with 1/4 cup puréed fruit.

The Best Oils for Cooking, and Oils to Avoid

Cold-pressed olive oil is delicious both in salad dressings and in savoury cooking. This oil has been used for thousands of years, and is a good choice if you only have one oil in the kitchen.

Olive oil can be replaced with safflower or sunflower oils for those looking for a cheaper alternative. These oils have not had as much traditional use as olive oil, and are high in omega 6, so it's important if you are using a lot of these oils to be eating plenty of foods high in omega 3, such as chia seeds, flaxseeds and hemp seeds, to correct the balance (see page 9).

There has been some debate over how oils handle the high temperatures involved in cooking, and much of this argument is in favour of coconut oil for use in baked dishes. Cold-pressed, unrefined coconut oil solidifies at a cold room temperature, making it ideal for replacing butter and margarine. To work with coconut oil, you'll first need to melt it by placing the jar of it in a larger bowl filled with hot water, so that the jar stands up and isn't on its side (water can leak into the jar if it falls over). If you need a larger amount of coconut oil, you will need to use boiling water. If you can't find coconut oil, it can be replaced in these recipes with vegan margarine.

For those avoiding genetically modified foods, the cooking oils that are usually genetically modified are canola (rapeseed), cottonseed, corn and soya. These are best replaced by olive oil.

Vegan Nutrition

I haven't provided calorie counts or detailed nutritional information for any of the recipes because I don't believe these can provide an accurate reflection on the qualities of a vegan wholefoods recipe. Reducing nutrition to numerical value results in homegrown vegetables being put on the same level as the products of industrial agriculture. With some research it's easy enough to tell the nutritional value of a recipe by looking at an ingredients list. I also don't wish to ruin the magic of cooking by making it overly scientific. That being said, there are a few things to watch out for in the vegan diet. I will not go into every nutrient that humans need, but will point out a few things that vegans need to be especially aware of. If you're eating a colourful variety of fruit and vegetables, including plenty of leafy greens, chances are that you're getting most of the nutrients you need. Here is a list of some nutrients that vegans struggle with, and how to counter that without resorting to synthetic vitamin pills.

Protein

Protein should be a part of every vegan meal. While there is protein in lots of vegetable sources, for many people it's important to include one high-protein source in every meal, which could be beans, lentils, nuts or seitan. A lack of protein is what makes a lot of vegetarians and vegans struggle with their diet, because they are often only exposed to risottos, vegetable stir-fries and other low-protein dishes that leave many appetites craving more, and find that they miss the satisfied 'full' feeling they used to get from a balanced meal. The main course recipes included in this book satisfy the protein needs of vegans, even during pregnancy and breastfeeding.

Raw and Lightly Cooked Foods

Many people overcook vegetables. I like to steam or sauté side-serves of vegetables until they're just cooked, but still crunchy. You can tell this by the change in colour in the vegetables. For example, when steaming or boiling broccoli, finish cooking as soon as the colour changes to a vibrant green. This only takes about two minutes. If you leave the steaming or sautéing until everything else in the meal is ready, then you have more chance of success with this, and ultimately more nutrients and texture. Adding raw and lightly cooked foods to meals not only provides a greater variety and quality of nutrients, but adds interest to a meal, with lighter, crunchier bites in between tastes of 'heavier' foods like seitan and legume dishes. It's as easy as making a garden salad or adding some raw kale to each plate of stew.

Vitamin B12

Vitamin B12 is something many vegans need to be aware of. If you cook with plenty of nutritional yeast (savoury yeast flakes) a couple of times a week, or regularly sprinkle it on your meals then you're probably getting enough of this in your diet. It is also sometimes found in fortified vegan milks. If you're not confident that you're getting it from these sources, then it may be a good idea to supplement with tablets.

Iodine can be found in sea vegetables; it is especially high in kelp, which is best bought in granule form to add nutrition to savoury dishes; it also adds depth to the flavours when used in small amounts, without making your food taste like sea vegetables. A small amount is all that is needed if eaten every day. I haven't included it as an ingredient in all my recipes because I don't wish to over-complicate things, but I would recommend adding a pinch of kelp granules per serve to any savoury meal once a day, especially if you are pregnant or breastfeeding.

Vitamin D3 is essential for calcium absorption; it can't be found naturally in any vegan food, but can be obtained by exposure to direct sunlight. Everyone is different in their ability to obtain enough vitamin D from sunlight, so if you plan on not taking any vitamin pills, it's probably best to get your vitamin D3 levels checked every now and then. Vitamin D3 pills vary in where it is sourced from and what vegan or non-vegan additives they contain, so it is worthwhile to check. The most cruelty-free (but still not strictly vegan) source is from lanolin, which is wool fat; this doesn't involve harming the sheep.

Calcium can be found in naturally high levels in certain sea vegetables, particularly lithothamnium cacareum (sold as Lifestream Natural Calcium), or as Aquamin, which is sometimes added to vegan milks. Many nuts, seeds, beans and vegetables such as collards, kale and broccoli have high levels of calcium.

Fats, and the essential fatty acids Omega 3 and 6

Fat is necessary for the human body to absorb vitamins and function healthily. It also contributes to a balanced meal by adding flavour along with providing sustained energy to keep the eater full for longer. Weight gain is caused by an excess of unused energy from food and can be fixed by using this energy for physical activity. I have included a low fat category in this book not because I believe a low fat diet is beneficial for all people, but to make it easier for people who have researched it and found that they need to be eating in this way for a time to find suitable recipes.

Omega 3 and 6 are found in some kinds of fat, and it's important to have a good balance between these. The modern diet is often very high in polyunsaturated oils which contain a lot of omega 6, with low levels of omega 3, and for the best health it is a good idea to correct this. A good balance can be obtained by eating chia seeds, flaxseeds, hempseeds and their cold-pressed oils to get extra omega 3, along with limiting your intake of oils which are high in omega 6.

To limit your intake of omega 6, it's best to use cold-pressed olive oil and coconut oil in place of other oils whenever possible, these are minimally processed oils that have been used traditionally for a long time and are much lower in omega 6 than other oils like sunflower, safflower and canola.

Flaxseed oil and ground flaxseeds go rancid at room temperature, so if you are buying these make sure they are refrigerated and that the flaxseed oil is cold-processed.

Iron

Getting enough iron for most vegans is not an issue at all. High levels can be found in leafy green vegetables, and cooking in cast iron cookware will also result in a high iron intake. Vitamin C is important for iron absorption, and this can often be found in the same vegetables that contain iron, or in fruits and apple cider vinegar. Legumes such as lentils, chickpeas and cannellini beans are another good source of iron, along with dark chocolate and a number of other delicious vegan foods. So if you are adding leafy greens to your meals or having at least one side-dish salad a day you should have no problems with this. Zinc is generally found in the same vegetable sources as iron, so deficiency in this is usually not an issue in a healthy vegan wholefoods diet.

Avoiding GMOs

Many people are concerned about the impacts genetically modified foods have on their health, and the health of future generations. Studies on animals have shown that those fed on genetically modified food had much higher rates of cancer, and that they and their descendants experienced fertility problems and more birth defects than non-GMO fed animals. Genetically modified crops are often engineered to withstand high doses of herbicides, or to create their own pesticide, and even as I write crops are being developed for the most cosmetic and unnatural of reasons, and not with our health in mind. Given that the methods used to grow genetically modified crops end up with the local wildlife and ecosystems being poisoned, it really goes against vegan ethics to be eating these crops.

Avoiding these products on an unprocessed wholefoods diet is easy, and only a matter of finding out which genetically modified crops are grown in which area, so you can be sure that by avoiding these products you are avoiding genetically modified food. Currently (2011) all organically certified products must be completely free of GMOs, so by making sure the sources of these products are organic, you are also avoiding GMOs. Many countries also have organisations around to help people avoid GMOs; for instance, in Australia there is the True Food Network, which publishes lists of companies which are boycotting GMOs, so you can be sure that if you are buying non-organic food, you are not supporting genetic engineering. Sometimes in processed foods the genetically modified oils (corn, cottonseed, soybean and canola) are simply labeled "vegetable oil". This book will help you to avoid GMOs by providing you with ideas and recipes for delicious meals and treats which can easily be fitted into busy lives, to reduce or completely eliminate dependence on processed food and takeaways.

Important Ingredients

Apple cider vinegar

Oils (Cold-pressed olive and coconut are the most important, see page 7).

Salt The less refined, the better. Salts that have a colour and a smell, such as Celtic sea salt, fleur de sel and Victorian lake salt are the best choices.

Vegan worcestershire sauce, coconut aminos or soy-free tamari - Some worcestershire sauces contain fish and soy, so be sure to check the ingredients. If it is labeled 'suitable for vegetarians', this will generally mean that it's OK for vegans too.

Tomato sauce or ketchup - I like to use sauces which are thick and bright, but not overly sweet. The more watery, chutney-style tomato sauces won't work so well in my recipes, so it's worth getting a more concentrated sauce for cooking, even if you don't like the taste of it on its own.

Chickpea flour (besan flour) - See page 7 (replacing eggs).

Gluten (vital wheat gluten) - for the seitan dishes.

Nutritional yeast (savoury yeast flakes) - This is essential for creating a 'cheese' flavour in dishes, along with adding extra savoury flavour and nutrition. It's worth tracking down over the internet if you can't find it in shops.

Wholemeal wheat flour - For yeast bread baking.

Barley flour, wholewheat pastry flour or wholemeal spelt flour - These are low gluten flours for baking sweet food, but can also be used for pretty much any purpose where flour is called for, except for making yeast breads. Barley flour is the best of these, and you may find that you need to use a teaspoon or two of extra water per cup of flour if you're using spelt or wholewheat pastry flour.

Rolled oats, steamed oats or quick oats

Nuts - Cashews or sunflower seeds, walnuts, almonds.

Grains - Brown rice, barley and quinoa.

Lentils - Red split and whole brown/green ones.

Canned or dried beans - Chickpeas, red kidney beans, borlotti or pinto beans, cannellini beans, black beans and 4 bean mix.

Canned tomatoes or fresh tomatoes

Canned coconut cream - I only use this in a couple of my recipes, but will usually cook one of these every couple of weeks, so I like to have a can in the cupboard at all times.

Wholemeal spaghetti, penne and lasagne sheets

Wholemeal mountain bread - A very thin, flat, rectangular bread (measures 21x24cm (8.2x9.4"). It is useful from anything from lasagnes to not-sausage rolls and party pies, you can use big tortillas instead if you can't find this.

Soy-free vegan milk - Rice and oat are the most commonly available.

Tahini (Unhulled is the best, and is sometimes known as sesame paste) or natural peanut butter - Only a couple of my recipes require tahini, but it is very high in calcium and a good addition to breads. Some peanut butters contain unnecessary additives, the best kinds contain peanuts and nothing else.

Organic cornmeal (polenta) or breadcrumbs (be sure to check the breadcrumb ingredients).

Sesame seeds - These are high in calcium and great for coating breads and also for sprinkling on top of savoury bakes. Unhulled, or mechanically hulled (chemical free) are the best choices.

Dried or fresh herbs - I use dried herbs in my recipes, these can be replaced by fresh herbs by using 2-4 times the amount called for, and adding it towards the end of the cooking rather than at the start. Oregano and thyme are the most important in this cookbook.

Spices - Cayenne pepper used minimally enhances the flavour of many savoury dishes. It is the pure dried and powdered form of the cayenne chilli pepper. If you can't find this, find another kind of powdered chilli, but be sure to check the ingredients that it's 100% chilli, and not a blend of spices. Other important spices are coriander, cumin, cloves, black pepper, turmeric, garam masala, paprika, nutmeg and cinnamon.

Cocoa powder

Rapadura or raw sugar - Rapadura is the healthier choice of these sugars, but more expensive and harder to find. To turn either of these into brown sugar add about a teaspoon of barley malt syrup, golden syrup or molasses per cup of sugar to the recipe. To turn into caster sugar or powdered sugar, grind in a food processor or coffee grinder, adding a teaspoon of tapioca flour per cup for powdered sugar. Raw and rapadura sugar work just as well in sweet dishes as the refined stuff, which is sometimes processed using animal products.

Barley malt syrup, molasses or golden syrup

Vanilla extract - The best stuff will be labeled 'natural' and contains real vanilla.

Maple syrup, agave nectar or other honey substitute - For use in salad dressings and more.

Baking powder and bicarb soda

Vegetables and fruit

Garlic - Local and organic is best, imported garlic is often bleached, irradiated and sprayed with chemicals.

Ginger - This will keep for a while if you keep it in open air, it's good to have on hand if you often make Indian food.

Onions or leeks

Salad greens (lettuce, mesclun, red russian or tuscan kale).

Cooking greens (e.g. kale, silverbeet (swiss chard), collards, spinach).

Cauliflower

Cabbage

Broccoli

Potatoes or swedes (rutabagas)

Sweet potatoes

Carrots

Lemons (lemon zest is used in a couple of these recipes, but lemon juice can mostly be replaced by apple cider vinegar)

Ingredients to source organically

If you're trying to avoid chemicals in food, a good general rule is to source organically grown fruits and vegetables when it's anything that you're going to eat the skin of, or fruit such as tomatoes, capsicums and peaches which have thin skins. Other vegetables to find organically grown are salad and cooking greens, potatoes and celery.

Cooking Tips

Oven Temperatures are given as a range, usually between 160-200c (320-390f). The lower temperature is for an efficient fan-forced oven, and the higher temperature is for a not-so-good oven. If you're cooking with a standard electric oven, try something in the middle of this range first.

Always make sure the oven is fully preheated before starting to bake anything.

Many of my savoury dishes involve sautéing. For best results heat two to three teaspoons of oil in the pan, then add the onion once the pan and the oil have heated up. You should be able to tell when it's hot enough by how quickly the oil moves around the pan when tipped, if it is slow then it's not ready, but once it is fast and the oil appears to be thinner than it was cold, then it is probably ready. Test this by sprinkling a tiny bit of water with your hands; if it quickly sizzles, then it's time to add the onion. Add the onion to this, usually at a medium-high heat, and stir it around, coating it in the oil. Continue to stir for a little longer. For best results stir it a lot until the onion has coloured up and is tender and smells tasty, this should only take a couple of minutes.

To shallow fry, heat the specified amount of oil (usually around 1/4-1/2 cm (1/8-1/4") in a frying pan over medium-high heat. Tilt the pan around as it heats up and note when it starts to move more freely. Test by placing a small piece of whatever you are cooking in the oil; it should sizzle straight away when it's ready.

Most stovetop dishes are generally cooked with the lids on, when left to simmer. This results in faster cooking, and more predictable results when cooking grains. If you don't have lids, you could cover the saucepans with plates.

For the best baked treats: When baking anything with cocoa in it, always grease and flour the tin. For most other dishes, brushing the tin with oil is fine, but if the tin is a fancy shape it is a good idea to flour it also, by putting a couple of tablespoons of flour into the greased tin, and tapping it around at all angles so that it is evenly sprinkled throughout the tin. Tap the tin upside down to get rid of excess flour.

To press a crust into a springform pan, divide the mixture into thirds. If it will be baked without a top, press 2/3 of the mixture into the bottom of the pan, right to the edges if you can. Take the other 1/3 and break into 8 pieces. Roll each piece into a mini-sausage shape and press into roughly 1/8 of the pan side per piece, joining it onto the rest of the crust. Press along the sides, raising it as high as you need it to go.

Kale is always used with the stem ripped off, to do this quickly, hold the stem in one hand and run your other hand along the edges, ripping off the leafy parts.

Cooking Grains and Beans

* When using canned beans, always drain and thoroughly rinse the beans before adding them to the recipe.

* All lentils called for in these recipes are measured dry, and the cooking times taken into account in the recipe. To speed up cooking times in some recipes you could use tinned brown lentils instead, giving a few more under 45 minute options.

* Never add salt to the cooking water of dry beans or lentils until they are cooked.

* Beans are generally measured in their cooked amounts. A 400g (14oz) tin is 1 1/2 cups of cooked beans.

Cooking Grains

To cook any grain, you first need to rinse it in cold water, then briefly drain. Put the grain and the required amount of cold water to a saucepan and bring it to the boil on a medium-high setting with the lid on. Once it is thoroughly boiling, reduce the heat to a low setting and simmer for the time specified.

For quinoa: 15 minutes. 1 part quinoa to 2 parts water.
For brown rice: 25-30 minutes. 1 part brown rice to 1 1/2 parts water.
For barley: 30-35 minutes. 1 part barley to 2 parts water.

Take the pan off the heat and leave it to sit with the lid on for 5-10 minutes to finish cooking.

Try not to take the lid off at all during the cooking process, as this will result in more of the water evaporating, and less soaking into the grains. Grains cooked this way do not need stirring during the cooking time.

Soaking and Cooking Beans

Quick soaking: Rinse the beans, then bring them and at least triple the amount of water to the boil. Boil rapidly for 2 minutes, then turn the heat off and leave for an hour with the lid on.

Overnight soaking: Rinse the beans and place in a bowl with at least three times their height in cold water. Leave to sit for 8-24 hours.

Cooking:
When the beans have finished soaking, drain and rinse. Cover with at least twice their height in cold water and bring to the boil. Boil rapidly for 5 minutes, then reduce the heat and simmer for the specified time. The times will vary depending on how long the beans have been soaked, their age, and how they've been stored.

Chickpeas: 1-2 hours
Borlotti beans: 1-2 hours
Red Kidney beans: 1- 2 hours
Cannelini beans: 45-90 minutes
Black (turtle) beans: 45-60 minutes
Split red lentils (no soaking required): 10-20 minutes
Whole brown/green lentils (no soaking required): 30-45 minutes
French puy lentils (black lentils) (no soaking required): 40-50 minutes

* Beans and lentils generally swell to 2 1/2 to 3 times their dry size once cooked. To cook enough beans to replace a 400g (14oz) tin, soak and cook 2/3 cup of dry beans, and you will have at least 1 1/2 cups of cooked beans.

* If dark froth develops on the surface of the water during cooking, discard as much of the froth as possible by skimming it off with a spoon.

The Process of Making Bread

Mixing: Yeast is dissolved in water, and then the flour added. Sometimes this will need to be kneaded a few times, to make sure that the flour is evenly mixed. Kneading is the process of folding the dough in half with your hands until all the flour is mixed. This can be done in the mixing bowl, or on a wet surface.

Rising: The rise is essential for the gluten to develop and form the best texture and taste. I like to make longer rising breads, because they taste better, use less yeast, and stay fresh for longer. During the rising time it's best to have the bowl covered by a tea towel or loose fitting lid that allows some air to escape.

Preheating the Pizza Stone: I strongly recommend using a pizza stone for bread baking. They don't cost much and don't take up much space in the kitchen. Using one of these means the the loaf will evenly cook, and the baking time will be more predictable. When using a pizza stone, you need it to heat in the oven first for at least half an hour, so that it can absorb a lot of heat. I've found that for the best results it is a good idea to preheat the oven to a higher heat than you will be baking the loaf at.

Shaping the Loaves: The easiest way to hand shape a loaf is to get a dinner plate and cover it in sesame seeds, semolina, cornmeal, or flour. Get the portion you want to form into a loaf and place it over this as a flat-ish circle. Take the sides of this circle and fold them up to form a log, flattening the seam. Place seam-side down on the preheated pizza stone.

Slashing the loaves: When the bread rises in the oven, it sometimes has to burst out of its formed shape. Having decorative slashes on the dough means that the bread will generally stay in its shape, rather than bursting out all over the place. The best way to slash a loaf is with a serrated bread knife, as soon as you've placed it on the pizza stone. Make a few cuts diagonally into the bread and shut the door immediately.

Baking: It's best to have the oven door shut for the entire time, so that a high temperature is maintained. It may take some practise to figure out how long bread takes to cook in your oven. You can generally tell if it looks cooked, and if you knock on the bottom of the loaf with your knuckles, it should sound hollow. If you're baking more than one loaf at once, you may find that the sides have touched during the baking, and that these sides aren't cooked, while the rest of the loaf is perfect. To fix this, turn off the oven, and turn the loaves so that the undercooked side is on the outside, and the cooked sides are touching. Leave them to bake in the residual heat, and to cool down in the oven.

Storing the loaves: The best way to store a loaf is in a paper bag, or wrapped in paper, so that no parts of the crust are exposed to the air. Make sure that the loaf has fully cooled before doing this.

Refreshing stale bread: If your bread is tasting a bit stale, you can refresh it by preheating the oven to 165c (325f), placing the bread in a paper bag and closing the bag, then pouring some water over the bag until the bag is soaked. You don't want to pour too much water over it, just enough to dampen the bag.

Place the bag in the oven until the bread has softened and warmed. This will take around 5 minutes for slices or rolls, or at least 20 minutes for loaves.

Wholegrain Baking Tips
• These doughs may not rise during the rising period as much as a refined flour dough, but in the oven they do rise and develop a nice texture.
• 100% wholemeal bread may take some getting used to, but once you're used to this bread, the nutritionally watered-down stuff from the shop will start to taste bland and unsatisfying.

Working with Fresh Yeast

Fresh, or compressed yeast can be kept in the fridge for about a week, or in the freezer for a month or more. To freeze, first crumble the block into the smallest pieces possible. To defrost, add this to the liquid portion of the mixture, and leave to sit until it defrosts. If the pieces are small it should only take a couple of minutes.

Slow-Rise Wholemeal Wheat Bread

Kitchen time 5 minutes
Resting time 16-60 hours
Baking time 35-60 minutes

NSI **LF NF** OGF

Makes 2 medium loaves

This is a good bread to make if you have a busy or unpredictable life. Each rise can take between eight and twenty hours and put in the fridge at any stage, to be baked within two weeks. It can also be sped up a little, to make the total time as little as 16 hours by doubling the amount of yeast and combining the first and second rise together. The long rise not only softens the wholemeal grain but makes it develop a unique taste similar to a subtle sourdough, without using any sugar or oil. This recipe makes two medium-sized, hand-shaped loaves. If you wish to make a third smaller portion that can be used for a pizza (page 18) fougasse (page 19) or for bread rolls for veggie burgers (pages 38-48), you can add an extra 1 cup of water and 2 1/2 cups of flour in the last rise.

Total ingredients
1/3 teaspoon fresh yeast, or 1/6 teaspoon dried
4 cups cold water
7 cups wholemeal wheat flour
2 teaspoons salt

First rise:
1/3 teaspoon fresh yeast, or 1/6 teaspoon dried
1 cup wholemeal wheat flour
1 cup cold water

Mix these together and set aside for 8-20 hours

Second rise:
2 cups cold water
3 cups wholemeal wheat flour

Mix this into the rest of the dough and set aside for 8-20 hours

Third rise:
2 teaspoons salt
1 cup cold water
3 cups wholemeal wheat flour

Mix this in thoroughly to the rest of the dough, it may need to be briefly kneaded to incorporate all the flour. Set aside for 8-20 hours.

To bake: Preheat the oven with a pizza stone in it to 230-260c (450-500f) or as hot as your oven will go. When the pizza stone has been in there for at least half an hour, shape the loaves into whatever shapes you wish, and coat in sesame seeds, cornmeal, or flour, making sure any cracks in the dough are on the bottom of the loaf. Place on the pizza stone, slash a few times with a bread knife, close oven door and reduce heat to 200-230c (390-450f).

Bake until the bottom of the loaves sound hollow when tapped, about 35-60 minutes.

Variations:
For rolls, follow the pizza stone preheating directions above, then take a chunk of dough, the size you would use for a pizza base, divide it in two and shape into whatever roll shape you'd like. Squash these down to be about 2cm (1") thick (they will rise in the oven), cover in sesame seeds, cornmeal or flour, and bake at 200-230c (390-450f) until they sound hollow when tapped on the bottom, about 10-15 minutes.

To make one of the loaves a fruit loaf, stretch it out to a flat rectangle, for rolling up, about 1cm (1/2") thick. Spread 1-3 tablespoons of barley malt syrup on this, and a handful or two of nuts, then fold in half. Sprinkle a couple of handfuls of dried fruit over this, then roll up and bake.

15

Spiced Fruit Loaf

A delicious loaf with a rising time that can be varied to suit your needs.

Kitchen time 5-10 minutes
Resting time 6-20 hours
Baking time 45- 60 minutes

Ingredients

NSI **LF NF** OGF

Makes 1 large loaf

Fruit mix:
1 1/2 cups dried fruit
2 cups water

Spiced dough:
1 1/2 cups cold water
2 teaspoons fresh yeast, or 1 teaspoon dried yeast
2 teaspoons salt
2 teaspoons cinnamon
1/2 teaspoon nutmeg
1/2 teaspoon cardamon (optional)
pinches of any other spice you would like eg. cloves, ginger
2-3 tablespoons barley malt syrup or sugar
2 tablespoons tahini or oil (melted coconut, olive or sunflower)
5 cups wholemeal wheat flour

extra 1 cup barley flour, wholemeal spelt flour, or extra wholemeal wheat flour,
for adding to the dough with the soaked fruit mix.

Method

In a small saucepan, bring the dried fruit and 2 cups of water to the boil. Take off the heat, and take out 3/4 cup of the water. Mix this with 1 1/2 cups cold water in a small bowl or measuring cup. Leave the fruit and the remaining water in the saucepan and set aside for at least 2 hours.

In a large mixing bowl, combine the yeast, salt, spices, barley malt and tahini to form a thick paste. Slowly add the water to this and mix until combined. Stir in the 5 cups of wholemeal wheat flour with a fork, continuing the mixing with your hands so that the flour is evenly incorporated.

The total time needed for rising this loaf is flexible, and anything between 6 hours and 20 hours will work.

*** Before adding the soaked fruit and the barley flour, the spiced dough mixture will need to rest for at least two hours. The fruit and barley flour can be added right at the end of the rising time and baked straight away, if that suits your schedule better. ***

After at least 2 hours have passed, add the fruit mixture and the barley flour to the spiced dough. Mix this until it's evenly combined and no traces of flour remain, then leave it to rise for the rest of the rising time.

When it has finished rising, preheat the oven with a pizza stone in it to 230-260 c (450-500f) or as hot as your oven will go. When the pizza stone has been in there for at least half an hour, shape the loaf into whatever shape you wish, and coat in sesame seeds, cornmeal or flour, making sure any cracks in the dough are on the bottom of the loaf. Place on the pizza stone, slash a few times with a bread knife, close the oven door and reduce heat to 200-230c (390-450f).
Bake until it sounds hollow when tapped on the bottom, about 45-60 minutes.

Fast Pizza Dough

Kitchen time 5-10 minutes
Resting time 30-60 minutes
Baking time 20-30 minutes

NSI **LF NF** OGF

Makes 1 pizza (2 serves)

Ingredients

1/4 cup water, for boiling
1/2 cup cold water
3 teaspoons fresh yeast, or 1 1/2 teaspoons dried yeast
1 tablespooon olive oil
1 1/2 cups wholemeal wheat flour
1/4 cup cornmeal (polenta) or more wholemeal wheat flour
optional tablespoon gluten
1/2 teaspoon salt

Method

Bring 1/4 cup water to the boil. Take off the heat and add the 1/2 cup cold water, the yeast. and the oil.

In a mixing bowl, combine the wholemeal wheat flour, cornmeal, gluten and salt. Add the water, yeast and oil to this, stirring to combine. Knead for 2-5 minutes, until the dough develops some elasticity.

Leave to rise for 30-60 minutes, while the oven heats up.

Preheat the oven with a pizza stone in it to 230-260 c (450-500f) or as hot as your oven will go. When the pizza stone has been in there for at least half an hour, roll or stretch out the dough, dusting the bottom with cornmeal. Place this on the pizza stone and bake for 5 minutes, until the top is just cooked. Add the pizza sauce (page 13) and toppings, and bake for another 15-25 minutes, until the toppings and sauce are hot.

Gluten-Free Potato Pizza

Kitchen time 5-10 minutes
Baking time 10-30 minutes

NSI **LF** (under 45 minutes)

Ingredients

Potatoes
Borlotti bean and kale pizza sauce (page 13)
Your favourite pizza toppings

Method

Boil and slice some potatoes.

Preheat the oven to 160-200c (320-390f).

Place the boiled and sliced potatoes as a thin layer on an oiled plate for each person.

Top them with the borlotti bean and kale pizza sauce (page 13) and your other favourite pizza toppings for a gluten-free meal without having to wait for pizza dough to rise.

Bake for 10-30 minutes, until the toppings are hot.

Borlotti Bean and Kale Pizza Sauce

While this hasn't been tested on vegetable-hating children, I suspect it's a good way to get them to eat leafy green vegetables. It adds heaps of protein and nutrition to a pizza, along with a rich taste that's more interesting than tomato paste-based sauces.

NSI **LF** OGF option
(under 45 minutes)

Makes enough for 2 pizzas
(4 serves)

Ingredients
1 1/2 cups cooked borlotti or pinto beans (1 400g (14oz) tin)
400g (14oz) tomatoes
2 teaspoons dried herbs (eg. oregano and thyme)
2 cloves garlic, or 1/4 an onion, optional
1/8-1/4 teaspoon cayenne pepper
1/2 teaspoon salt
2-3 big leaves of kale or other leafy green

Method
Blend all ingredients except the kale in a food processor or blender until fairly smooth.

Add the kale and blend until it's finely chopped.

Toppings for pizzas: Cauliflower may sound weird, but it really is delicious when it's chopped into tiny florets. Zucchini, olives, pineapple, capsicum, mushrooms, beans, cabbage, tomatoes, onion, nuts or precooked vegetables such as potato, sweet potato and pumpkin. Slices of avocado make a good replacement for cheese, or you could use cashew cheese (page 60) or servo style cheesy sauce (page 76).

Cannellini Bean and Kale Fougasse

Kitchen time 5-10 minutes
Baking time 20 minutes

NSI **LF option NF** OGF

A foccacia-like bread filled with a simple mixture of thyme, beans and kale.

Ingredients

1 recipe fast pizza dough (page 17), or one 400g (14oz) chunk of bread dough
1 1/2 cups cooked cannellini beans (1 400g (14oz) tin)
1/2 teaspoon salt
2 teaspoons dried thyme, or 2 tablespoons fresh
2 cups finely chopped kale or other leafy green

Makes 1 flat bread
(2 meal-sized serves)

Method

Preheat the oven with a pizza stone in it to 230-260 c (450-500f) or as hot as your oven will go. Prepare the dough according to the directions on page 17 and leave it to rise.

Mash the cannellini beans together with the salt, thyme and kale until evenly mixed.

When the oven has finished preheating (and the pizza stone has been in there for at least half an hour), stretch the dough out into a square the width of your pizza stone on a surface covered with cornmeal or semolina. Place the bean mixture on one rectangular half of this, leaving room around the edges to seal it together.

Press the edges together to seal. Sprinkle with some extra thyme if you'd like.

Place on the heated pizza stone and make diagonal slashes with a bread knife to expose the kale and bean filling. Reduce the heat to 200-230c (390-450f) and bake for 20 minutes.

Cinnamon Scrolls

The bakery version of these is typically iced, but these are just as delicious (and healthier) without icing.

Kitchen time 10-15 minutes
Resting time 2-3 hours
Baking time 10-15 minutes

LF option NF OGF

Makes around 9 (4 serves)

Ingredients

For the dough:
1/4 cup vegan milk, for boiling
1/2 cup vegan milk, cold
3 teaspoons fresh yeast, or 1 1/2 teaspoons dried yeast
1/4 cup sugar
1/4 cup apple purée or oil
1/4 cup chickpea flour (besan)
1 1/2 cups wholemeal wheat flour
1 cup whole barley, spelt or wheat flour
a pinch of salt

For the filling:
1 1/2 tablespoons oil or apple purée
1/3 - 1/2 cup raw sugar or rapadura
1 1/2 teaspoons cinnamon
optional 1 teaspoon barley malt syrup
optional 1 medium apple, finely diced

Method

To make the dough, bring 1/4 cup of vegan milk to the boil. Remove from the heat, and add the other 1/2 cup of vegan milk, along with the yeast, sugar and apple purée or oil.

In a mixing bowl, combine the flours and salt. Mix the vegan milk mixture into this and knead a few times, until the dough develops some elasticity.

Leave in a bowl, covered with a tea towel, for 2-3 hours.

When the dough has finished rising, roll it out to a square, about 3/4 of a centimetre thick (1/3 inch). Brush with the oil and then sprinkle with the sugar, cinnamon and the apple. Drizzle with the barley malt syrup, then roll up and seal by pressing the seam into the rest of the dough.

Carefully cut into 2 1/2 cm (1 inch) slices, and place them on a greased baking sheet.

Heat the oven to 180-220c (350-430f). When the oven has finished heating up, bake the scrolls for 10-15 minutes, until golden. Serve hot or cold.

Doughnuts

When these are served hot they taste almost exactly like the traditional deep-fried version, but with way more nutrition and less fat.

Kitchen time 10-15 minutes
Resting time 2-4 hours
Baking time 10-15 minutes

LF option NF OGF

Makes 8-16 (4 serves)

Ingredients

For the dough:
100ml (3.4oz) vegan milk, for boiling
200ml (6.7oz) vegan milk, cold
2 teaspoons fresh yeast, or 1 teaspoon dried
75ml (2.5oz) oil or apple purée
1 1/2 cups wholemeal wheat flour
1 3/4 cups flour (barley, wholemeal spelt or wholewheat pastry)
1/4 cup chickpea flour (besan)
1/3 cup raw sugar or rapadura
a pinch of salt

1/4 cup strawberry jam, if you're making jam doughnuts

extra oil, for brushing before baking

For the cinnamon sugar coating:
extra oil, for coating doughnuts after baking
1/2 cup sugar, ground to resemble castor sugar
1 teaspoon cinnamon

Method

In a small saucepan, bring 100ml (3.4oz) of the vegan milk to the boil. Take off the heat, then stir though the remaining 200ml (6.7oz) of cold vegan milk. Stir in the yeast and the oil or apple purée.

In a big mixing bowl, combine the flours, sugar and salt until evenly mixed. Add the vegan milk, yeast and oil or apple purée, stirring, and then kneading to combine. Continue to knead for another 5 minutes, until the dough develops some elasticity. Leave in a bowl, covered with a tea towel, in a fairly warm spot for two to four hours.

When you're ready to bake the doughnuts, preheat the oven to 180-220c (350-430f).

To make jam doughnuts: Divide the mixture into 8 pieces. Roll each one into a ball, and then flatten to about 1cm (1/2") thick. Place a teaspoon full of jam in the middle of this, then pinch the edges out, to flatten them even more. Completely cover the jam with the thin dough by working in a circle, folding a little over at a time. Place seam-side down on a greased baking sheet and brush the top with some extra oil. Repeat for the remaining doughnuts that you wish to bake now.

To make regular doughnuts: Divide the mixture into 8 or 16 pieces. Turn each piece into a sausage shape, then press the ends together to turn into a doughnut, leaving plenty of space in the middle for the hole. Place on a greased baking sheet and brush with oil.

When the oven has heated up, bake the doughnuts for around 10 minutes, or until golden.

While the doughnuts are baking, prepare the cinnamon sugar by combining 1/2 cup raw sugar or rapadura in the food processor with a teaspoon of cinnamon. Blend until it resembles caster sugar (fine, but not as fine as icing sugar).

Brush each cooked doughnut with oil, then roll in cinnamon sugar. Serve hot.

Leftover Tips: The unbaked doughnuts can be refrigerated for a few days, or frozen for a few months.

STEWS, CURRIES, DUMPLINGS
AND OTHER STOVETOP RECIPES

Briami with Chickpeas

NSI **LF**
(under 45 minutes)

Makes 6 serves

Ingredients

500g (17oz) eggplants (2 medium ones)
800g (28oz) diced tomatoes (2 cans)
4 medium zucchini
500g (17oz) potatoes (5 medium ones)
1 large bulb of garlic, or 3 small ones
3 cups of cooked chickpeas (2 400g/14oz tins)
salt, to taste, and a little olive oil if you want
optional 1 cup finely chopped parsley

This is my one-pot main course version of the Greek briami. It is traditionally baked in a covered casserole dish in the oven, but I think it tastes just as good slowly simmered on the stove in a large pot. With some chickpeas added for protein, it makes a delicious main dish served over some cooked grains, such as barley (not gluten free) or quinoa, with a salad.

Method

Slice the eggplant into slices about one inch thick, sprinkle salt on them and leave them to sit for at least 15 minutes.

Slice the zucchinis and potatoes into bite-sized pieces.

Take the skin off each clove of garlic by putting the flat side of a chef knife against it, then putting some pressure on it, to slightly crush the clove, then slice off the 'root' end of it, taking the rest of the skin with it. Chop each clove into halves or quarters if you wish.

Put the tomatoes, chickpeas, garlic, zucchini and potatoes in a stockpot or large saucepan on a medium-high heat.

Rinse the salt off the eggplant and squeeze out any excess water. Chop into bite-sized pieces and add to the pot. Put the lid on the pot and bring to the boil. Reduce heat and simmer for at least half an hour, stirring every now and then.

Leftover tips: Briami is traditionally served at room temperature, and this version is just as nice served as a packed lunch with some bread and salad. As a hot meal it can be stored for a few days in the fridge and slowly reheated over the stove.

Two Lentil Dahl

When this is served with potatoes it satisfies cravings for potatoes and gravy, but in a much healthier way. The red lentils break down to form a thick gravy, while the brown lentils absorb flavour and make for some variety in texture. If you've only ever eaten dahl as a watery soup before, give this one a try and you may be surprised at how tasty and filling it is.

Ingredients

1 medium onion, diced
2 cloves garlic, finely chopped
2 heaped tablespoons of ginger, finely chopped
1 teaspoon coriander, ground
1 teaspoon cumin, ground
1/2 teaspoon cloves, ground
2 teaspoons turmeric
1/4 teaspoon cayenne pepper
1 cup dry split red lentils
1 cup dry brown lentils
7 cups water
1 teaspoon salt

Method

Sauté the onion until soft. Add the garlic and the ginger and stir for a minute longer, then add the spices and stir for another minute over low heat.

Add the lentils and water and bring to the boil. Reduce the heat and simmer for 30 minutes, then stir through the salt.

This is delicious poured on top of baked or mashed potatoes with raw kale.

Nightshade-free option: Omit the cayenne pepper, and serve with some cooked grains instead of potatoes.

Himalayan Barley and Vegetable Stew

A warming and spicy stew.

LF
(under 45 minutes)

Makes 6 serves

Ingredients

1 1/2 cups barley, rinsed
6 cups water
10 small-medium potatoes (800g/28oz), chopped into bite-sized pieces
3 medium onions, cut into wedges
1-2 capsicums (peppers), chopped into smallish pieces (optional)
3/4 cup finely chopped ginger
4 big cloves of garlic, finely chopped
1-2 chillies, finely chopped, or 1-2 teaspoons cayenne pepper
1 heaped dinner plate full of chopped veggies (fairly fast cooking ones like cauliflower, broccoli, carrot, cabbage, green beans etc)
3 cups cooked chickpeas (two 400g (14oz) tins)
1 large mixing bowl full of greens (about 9 big leaves silverbeet or kale), ripped into small pieces
zest and juice of 1 large lemon
1/2-2/3 cup of coconut aminos or soy-free tamari
salt, to taste
mung bean sprouts, to serve

Method

Put the barley and water in a large saucepan and bring to the boil. Simmer for 15-20 minutes, then add the potatoes. Simmer for another 20 minutes. Do not drain.

The next part of this recipe is very quick to cook, so it's a good idea to have all the ingredients prepared.

Heat a little oil in a stockpot or very big saucepan over a high heat. Add the onion and stir-fry for a couple of minutes, breaking up the wedges, until lightly and evenly cooked and fragrant. Stir through the capsicum, ginger, garlic and chilli, then add the vegetables and chickpeas (but not the greens). Continue to stir-fry for another 5 minutes, then add the potato and barley mixture, along with the greens. Stir these through until it's boiling and the vegetables are cooked, then add the lemon and the coconut aminos. Top each serving with a handful of sprouts.

Gluten-free option: Use brown rice instead of barley.

Hearty Lentil Borscht

Ingredients

NSI **LF NF**
(under 45 minutes)

Makes 6 serves

1 onion, finely chopped
optional 250g (9oz) finely chopped mushrooms
3 large beetroots: 2 diced, 1 grated
1 large swede (rutabaga) or turnip, diced (use carrot or extra beetroot if you don't have either of these)
1 1/2 - 2 cups of dry brown lentils
10-11 cups of water
Optional soy-free tamari, coconut aminos or vegan worcestershire sauce to taste (I use around 2-6 tablespoons)
Apple cider vinegar, to taste (I use around 1-4 tablespoons)
salt, to taste

Method

In a stockpot or large saucepan, sauté the onion and mushrooms until soft. Add the rest of the ingredients and bring to the boil.

26 Reduce heat and simmer for 30-40 minutes, until the beetroot and swede are soft. Adjust seasonings and serve with cashew sour cream (page 60).

Sweet, Sour and Spicy Chickpea Curry

Kitchen time 5 minutes
Cooking time 5 minutes

NSI **LF** OGF
(under 45 minutes)

Makes 4 serves

This curry has so much flavour it's almost like a chutney. I think it makes a good meal served with oven-baked pakoras (page 81) and brown rice, with some raw fruit or vegetables on the side. Made this way, it serves four.

Ingredients

1 teaspoon coriander, ground
1 teaspoon cumin seeds, crushed
pinch of cloves, ground
400g (14oz) tin diced tomatoes
3 cups cooked chickpeas (2 400g (14oz) cans)
2 tablespoons sultanas (raisins)
4 tablespoons (or to taste) apple cider vinegar or lemon juice
cayenne pepper, to taste (I use about 3/4-1 teaspoon)
2 teaspoons worcestershire sauce, optional
1 teaspoon garam masala
salt, to taste

Method

Heat the coriander, cumin and cloves in a pan for a minute or so, being careful not to burn. Add everything except the garam masala, bring to the boil and simmer for at least five minutes. Stir through the garam masala right at the end of the cooking, and adjust the other seasonings to taste.

Chili Con Lentils

Ingredients

3 medium onions
2 teaspoons coriander, ground
cayenne pepper, to taste
4 teaspoons paprika
3 teaspoons oregano (dried)
1.2kg (42oz) diced tomatoes
1 1/2 cups dry brown or puy lentils
1/2 cup dry split red lentils
4 cups water
1 tablespoon red wine vinegar or apple cider vinegar
salt, to taste
4 1/2 cups cooked red kidney or black beans (three 400g (14oz) tins)
1 tablespoon cocoa, optional

Method

Sauté the onion in a stockpot until fragrant, about 3 minutes. Add the spices and stir for 30 seconds. Add the tomatoes, oregano, water, lentils, salt and vinegar. Bring to the boil and simmer for 30 minutes. Add the beans and simmer for 10 minutes, add the cocoa and some fresh parsley if you have it (and some kale for extra nutrition, if you want) and serve. I like to serve this with barley or brown rice and some cashew sour cream (page 60)

Korma

A mildly spiced and creamy curry, complimented really well by the addition of sweet potatoes. Delicious served with cooked grains, and maybe some parathas (page 81)

Kitchen time 10 minutess
Cooking time 30 minutes

NSI **LF NF option**
(under 45 minutes)

Makes 6 serves

Ingredients
2 teaspoons coriander, ground
1 teaspoon cumin seeds
1 teaspoon ground cumin
2 teaspoons turmeric
1/2 teaspoon cloves, ground
1/2 teaspoon black pepper, ground
1/4 - 1 teaspoon cayenne pepper, to taste

1-3 medium onions, diced or in quarter moons
2 tablespoons finely chopped ginger
3 dinner plates of chopped vegetables (e.g. sweet potato, potato, cauliflower, swede (rutabaga), cabbage, pumpkin, carrot)
4 1/2 cups cooked chickpeas, kidney beans or black beans (3 400g (14oz) cans),
1 400g (14oz) can coconut cream (or 2 cans of coconut milk)
4 1/2 cups water (use 3 cups if using coconut milk)
optional 1/2 - 3/4 cups raw almonds
salt, to taste

Method
Prepare the first seven spices and set aside.

Chop the onion and ginger, then sauté the onion for a couple of minutes until soft. Add the ginger and sauté for another minute. Add the spices, stir for 30-60 seconds, then add the water and coconut cream.

Add the rest of the ingredients and bring to the boil. Reduce heat and simmer for 20-30 minutes, until the vegetables are tender. Stir through some kale or silverbeet for a couple of minutes for extra nutrition.

Nightshade-free option: Omit the cayenne pepper and don't use potato or any other vegetable from the nightshade family.

Tibetan Potato and Chickpea Curry

Kitchen time 10 minutes
Cooking time 30 minutes

NSI **LF** (under 45 minutes)

Makes 5 to 6 serves

Ingredients

1 medium onion, chopped into quarter moons
1 heaped tablespoon of chopped ginger
a couple of cloves of garlic, optional
1 1/2 teaspoons coriander, ground
pinch of cayenne pepper
1/2 teaspoon black pepper
650-700g potatoes, cut into bite-sized chunks
800g (28oz) diced tomatoes (2 cans)
2 cups water
5 large button mushrooms, chopped into small pieces
3 cups cooked chickpeas (2 400g (14oz) tins)
2 teaspoons apple cider vinegar
salt, to taste

Method

Sauté the onion on medium-high heat until golden and soft. Add the ginger and spices and stir for another 30 seconds.

Add the rest of the ingredients and bring to the boil. Reduce the heat and simmer, covered, for 30 minutes, or until the potatoes are tender.

Leftover tips: The last leftover portion can be made into a delicious noodle soup for two by adding another 5 chopped mushrooms, 1/2 a head of steamed broccoli, 2 serves (200g (7oz) dry weight) cooked spaghetti, 1/2 teaspoon black pepper, 1 teaspoon ground coriander, 2 teaspoons fresh ginger, a cup or two of water and a little extra salt, along with two handfuls of cashews or other nuts.

Hungarian Goulash with Dumplings

NSI **LF** (under 45 minutes)

Makes 6-8 serves

Ingredients
For the Goulash:
1 onion
250g (9oz) chopped mushrooms, optional
3 tablespoons paprika
2 litres water (2.1 quarts)
1/4 teaspoon black pepper
3 teaspoons caraway seeds
1 to 1 1/2 teaspoons salt, to taste
6 cups mixed beans (4 400g (14oz) tins)
2 medium potatoes, diced

Dumplings for two serves:
1 cup of wholemeal wheat flour
1 teaspoon baking powder
1/4 cup fresh parsley
2 tablespoons oil (melted coconut or olive)
1/2 cup vegan milk

Method
Sauté the onion (and mushroom, if using) over medium-high heat for a couple of minutes, until soft. Take off the heat and stir through the paprika. Add the rest of the ingredients (except the dumplings), bring to the boil, and simmer for 25 minutes, covered, until the potatoes are tender.

To make the dumplings, first mix the dry ingredients together, then add the rest of ingredients, kneading to combine. Shape into 6-8 balls and place on top of the simmering goulash for fifteen to twenty minutes, covered. This dumpling recipe makes enough for two serves, which I make up fresh every time the goulash is reheated. Alternatively, it can be served over pasta or with bread.

Low fat option: Serve with pasta or bread instead of the dumplings.

Gluten-free option: Use a gluten-free flour blend in the dumplings, or serve with gluten free pasta.

Thai Yellow Curry

While not traditional, this curry satisfies cravings for Thai food using ingredients that I usually have in the kitchen

Ingredients

2 small-medium onions, chopped
1-2 tablespoons finely chopped ginger
3-4 cloves finely chopped garlic
2 teaspoons coriander, ground
2 teaspoons turmeric
cayenne pepper, to taste
1 heaped dinner plate fast cooking vegetables, chopped (cauliflower, carrot, green beans, cabbage etc)
3-4 cups hot water
1 400g (14oz) tin coconut cream
3 cups cooked chickpeas (2 400g (14oz) tins)
salt, to taste
zest of one lemon
juice of half a lemon, or apple cider vinegar to taste
2-3 cups chopped broccoli or greens

Method

If serving this with a grain, get that cooking first, and start cooking the curry when the grains only have about 10 minutes to go.

Chop up all the vegetables and prepare the ingredients.

If serving this with pasta, put the pasta into boiling water now.

On high heat, stir fry the onion for a couple of minutes, until fragrant and tender. Add the ginger, garlic, coriander, turmeric, cayenne and the heaped dinner plate of quick cooking vegetables. Stir fry for a couple more minutes, then add the water, coconut cream and chickpeas. Cook until the vegetables are tender, but not mushy, about 5-7 minutes.

Add the salt, lemon zest and juice, and the greens. Stir through until the greens are cooked to your preference, about a 30-60 seconds for greens, or 2-3 minutes for broccoli.

Red lentil Bolognese

A really fast, simple and healthy recipe. For variety, you could add some chopped olives towards the end of cooking, along with extra cayenne pepper and garlic for more of a 'puttanesca' style sauce.

NSI **LF**
(under 45 minutes)

Ingredients

water for cooking
2/3 cup dry split red lentils
Wholemeal spaghetti or other pasta for two (200g (7 oz) dry weight)
1 recipe marinara sauce (page 61)
Kale or other leafy greens, optional

Serves 2

Method

Bring a big pot of water to the boil, do not add salt to the water.

While you're waiting for the water to boil, prepare the marinara sauce according to the directions on page 61

Add the lentils to the water and bring to the boil, if your lentils tend to take longer than 15 minutes to cook, then leave them in the pot for a couple of minutes longer; if not, add the pasta when the lentils are boiling and cook until tender but not mushy, about 13 minutes, or as long as it says on the packet.

Drain the pasta and lentils, and add them and the greens to the marinara sauce, stirring through until it's evenly mixed. Serve right away.

Gluten free option: Use gluten-free pasta

Pierogi with Simple Borscht

Kitchen time 45 minutes
Total time 1 1/2 hours

These delicious Polish dumplings take a lot more time and effort than most of my recipes, but the results are worth it. I think this works really well as two meals, to serve two of us I make the lentil filling for the first meal, and then for the second meal I make the cauliflower mixture, filling the pierogi with the leftover lentil mix first, and then filling the rest of the dumplings with the cauliflower mix. If you're cooking for more than two people, it's easy enough to just double or triple everything and do the same.

GF option NSI option LF
NF OGF option

Makes 4 serves

Ingredients
For the pierogi dough:
2 cups wholemeal wheat flour
1/2 teaspoon salt
1/2 cup cashew sour cream (page 60)
1/2 cup water

Lentil filling: (NSI LF NF)
1 cup dry brown lentils
1 medium onion, diced
2-4 tablespoons cashew sour cream (page 60)
ripped or chopped leafy greens, chives and parsley to taste (I use around three big leaves of kale)

Cauliflower and cheese filling: (NF OGF option)
1/3 of a small-medium cauliflower (around 350g (12oz) of florets)
1/2 cup sunflower seeds or cashews
1/4 cup nutritional yeast (savoury yeast flakes)
1/2 cup water
3/4 teaspoon salt
1 teaspoon apple cider vinegar
optional parsley, chives and leafy greens to taste

Borscht
(NSI LF NF)
1 small onion
3 medium beetroots, grated
4 cups of water
1 teaspoon salt
1 tablespoon apple cider vinegar

No special ingredient option: Use the lentil filling
Gluten-free option: Use a gluten free flour blend instead of wheat flour.
Onion- and garlic-free option: Use the cauliflower and cheese filling, not adding any chives to the mixture.

Method

If you're making the lentil filling, first bring 1 cup of lentils and at least 3 cups of water to the boil. Reduce the heat and simmer for half an hour, or until tender.

Make the cashew sour cream, following the instructions on page 60.

To make the pierogi dough: Mix the salt and flour together, then in a separate bowl mix up the sour cream and the water. Add the wet ingredients to the dry, and knead until evenly combined. Leave to rest for at least half an hour. While this is resting, you can prepare the pierogi filling and the borscht.

For the lentil filling: Sauté the onion over medium-high heat until golden and fragrant, about five minutes. Stir through the other ingredients to combine, then take off the heat.

This makes enough to fill around 2/3 of the pierogi dough. If you would like to make this to fill all of them, simply cook an additional 1/2 cup of dry brown lentils.

For the cauliflower and cheese filling: Steam the cauliflower for 5-7 minutes, until tender.

In a high speed blender, combine the sunflower seeds, nutritional yeast, water, salt and vinegar. Blend until smooth. Add 1/4 of the cooked cauliflower (about 2/3 of a cup, finely chopped) and 1/3 of a cup of water to the blender, and blend for another minute or so.

Finely chop the rest of the cooked cauliflower and place in a bowl. Add about 2/3 of the blended mixture, along with any finely chopped herbs or leafy greens.

This will make enough mixture to fill half the pierogi. To make enough to fill all of them, use all the blended mixture, and add 1 1/2 cups of cooked cannellini beans (1 400g (14oz) tin) to the mixture.

Any leftovers of this filling are delicious served with pasta the next day.

For the borscht: Sauté the onion over medium-high heat until golden and fragrant, about five minutes. Add the rest of the ingredients and bring to the boil. Reduce heat and simmer for at least ten minutes.

To assemble and cook the pierogi: When you have the pierogi filling and the borscht ready, and the dough has rested for at least half an hour, take half of the dough (or a quarter if you're cooking 1 serve), and roll it out fairly thinly, about 1/4-1/2 a centimetre. Take a drinking glass or mug and use this to cut circles out of the dough. Roll each circle out even more thinly. Place some filling on one side of each circle (I use about 1 to 2 tablespoons, but it will depend on how big the circles are). Make sure there is enough space around the edges to close the circle properly. Fold the circle in half to enclose the filling, then press the edges together. Set these aside, and repeat for the rest of the dough if you are preparing more than two serves of pierogi.

The rolling out and filling process will take about half an hour for all four serves. The filled pierogi can be refrigerated or frozen at this point.

While the pierogi are being filled, bring a big pot of water to the boil over a high heat. When it's at a rolling boil, add the pierogi. They should hopefully all sink to the bottom, sometimes they don't. Put the borscht into the soup bowls while you wait for the pierogi to cook.

When all the pierogi have risen to the top of the pot (this should take only a couple of minutes), drain them: Serve straight away, or sauté in a little oil.

Ravioli with Walnut, Lentil and Olive Filling

This ravioli is the result of a special night that I wanted to make a special meal for. While many special meals involve several different courses or dishes and a lot of time in the kitchen, this one is nutritious, filling and interesting enough to be served with a simple garden salad as a one course meal. Like many of my recipes, the various mixtures which make this dish can be stored in the fridge to create a second meal for two (or three more meals for one). Like pierogi, the ravioli can be filled beforehand and kept in the fridge or freezer, making it a good choice for an impressive meal to serve to guests.

Kitchen time: 30-45 minutes
Total time 60-75 minutes

NF option
OGF option

Makes 4 serves

Ingredients
For the filling:
3/4 cup dry brown lentils
1/4 cup barley (use brown rice for gluten free)
water for boiling
1 cup walnuts
1 tablespoon nutritional yeast (savoury yeast flakes)
1 clove garlic
pinch of cayenne
salt to taste
2 cups radish leaves, or another leafy green such as rocket or kale
1 teaspoon lemon juice of apple cider vinegar
9 pitted olives (I use kalamata)

For the pasta dough:
2 cups wholemeal wheat or semolina flour
1/2 cup chickpea flour (besan)
3/4 teaspoon salt
1 cup water

For the sauce:
1 double recipe marinara sauce (page 61), or any other pasta sauce of your choice
3-4 big leaves of kale or silverbeet (chard), torn into small pieces (optional)
Additional chopped olives, and fresh oregano to serve (optional)

Gluten-free option: Use a gluten free flour blend instead of the wheat flour in the pasta. Use brown rice instead of barley in the filling.
Nightshade-free option: Omit the cayenne pepper from the filling, and serve with a nightshade-free sauce, such as some puréed roast vegetables or pumpkin soup.
Onion- and garlic-free option: Omit the garlic from the filling, and serve with an onion- and garlic-free sauce.

Leftover tips: The ravioli can be filled ahead of time and left in the fridge or freezer until you need them; the dough, filling and sauce all keep well in the fridge for a few days.

Method

First bring the lentils and barley to the boil over a medium-high heat. Reduce the heat and simmer for about half an hour, until the lentils are tender and the barley is cooked.

While that is boiling, prepare the pasta dough by mixing all the dry ingredients together, breaking up any lumps. Stir through the water and knead until evenly mixed. Set aside for at least 15 minutes.

Prepare the marinara sauce according to the directions on page 60, leave it simmering on the stove on the lowest setting.

If you're serving it with a salad, prepare all the ingredients and the dressing now, but don't mix until the last minute.

When the lentils and barley have finished cooking, thoroughly drain them and make the rest of the filling by grinding the walnuts in a food processor with the nutritional yeast, garlic, salt and cayenne, until they're at a pesto consistency (small, even pieces). Add the radish leaves, lemon juice and olives and continue to blend, until the greens are in small, even pieces. You may have to take the lid off and stir once or twice, to evenly distribute the leaves.

Mix this mixture together with the drained lentils and barley, and prepare the pasta for filling. While you prepare your pasta, bring a big pot of water to the boil.

Depending on how much time you want to spend making the ravioli, you can either fill them as you do with pierogi, by rolling out half the dough at a time (or a quarter, for a single serve), cutting circles out with a cup, rolling them thinner, and then filling half, folding the other half over and sealing. If you want faster ravioli, you can use 1/4 of the dough at a time, to create serves of 2 big raviolis each. These are more prone to breaking, but as you can see in the photo above, they still look delicious and impressive.

To make the big ravioli, take 1/4 of the dough at a time and roll out as thin as you are comfortable working with. Cut through the middle, to create 2 thin rectangles. Place some filling in one half of the rectangles, leaving plenty of room around the edges for sealing, brush some water over the edges, fold the non-filled half over and seal by pressing together, rolling the edges over if you wish. Dust with flour and set aside while you prepare the rest of them using the same method.

When all the raviolis are prepared, place them in the boiling water for about three to five minutes. While they are boiling you can assemble a side salad from pre-prepared ingredients. Drain the ravioli, place a portion of marinara sauce on each plate, then top with the ravioli and garnish with herbs if you wish.

BURGERS, PATTIES
AND THINGS TO SERVE ON BREAD

Burger and Patty Tips

If you wish to flip the burgers during cooking, only do it once, and do it at least 3/4 of the way through the cooking time.

All the burger and patty mixtures will keep well in the fridge for a few days, and all except for the mushroom and oat rissoles can be frozen for a few months.

To make baked hash browns as burger buns: grate 400g (14oz) of potatoes or sweet potatoes, this is around 3 or 4 medium sized potatoes. Place in a tea towel and squeeze out as much liquid as you can. It should measure around 2 1/4 cups after squeezing.

Stir through 1/4 cup chickpea flour and 1/2 a teaspoon salt, then add 3-4 tablespoons of vegan milk, stirring until evenly combined.

Brush a lined baking sheet with oil, then divide the mixture into 4, and spread each one thinly in a circle. Bake for 20 minutes, flipping over for the last 5 minutes. Serves 2.

Burgers with The Lot
NF option (under 45 minutes option)

A healthy vegan version of the typical Australian chip shop burger, this works best with a mildly flavoured burger, to make the most of the toppings.

To make burgers with the lot, prepare any burger or seitan recipe (lentil burgers, page 41, work best), along with some bread rolls, or baked hash browns (see 'burger and pattie tips', this page), and some cashew cheese (page 60). Sauté 1-2 onions per person over medium high heat until tender, then turn down heat to low and continue to stir every so often, until tender and fragrant.

Spread the cashew cheese on the bread or hash browns, top with slices of fresh tomato (if in season), sautéed onion, sliced canned or boiled beetroot, salad and tomato or barbeque sauce. Pineapple can be used in place of the beetroot for a delicious 'Hawaiian' burger.

Gluten-free option: Use baked hash browns instead of bread rolls.

39

Cheezeburger

Prepare any burger or seitan recipe. Steaks made from the baked seitan recipe (page 50) work really well, lentil burgers and spicy black bean patties are good choices, too.

Prepare some baked hash browns (page 39) or a bread roll per person, along with some cashew cheese (page 60).

Spread cashew cheese on one side of each hash brown or halved bread roll, and top one side with a layer of gherkin slices (pickles), some chopped onion (optional), salad greens, the burger, and some tomato sauce (optional).

Seitan Schnitzel and Mayo Burger

NF OGF (under 45 minutes)

Avocado mayo (page 59) works best for this burger, but any kind of vegan mayonnaise, including the almond mayo recipe on page 60 will also be tasty.

Ingredients:
Bread rolls, or baked hash browns (page 39)
Seitan schnitzels (page 54)
Avocado mayo (1 recipe makes enough for two burgers, page 59) or almond mayo (page 60)
Salad greens

Method:
Prepare the seitan schnitzel for as many people as you want to make this for, along with the bread rolls or hash browns. When it's almost ready, prepare the avocado mayo. Spread the mayo on the bread, top with salad, then the schnitzel, put any extra mayo on top of the schnitzel.

Haggis Burgers

NF option

Prepare the haggis mixture on page 74. Add 2/3 cup chickpea flour and 2/3 cup water to the mixture to make four huge or six medium burgers. Bake for 30-40 minutes.

Seitan BLT

OGF (under 45 minutes)

Ingredients:
Bread slices or rolls
Easy baked seitan (page 50), 1/4 recipe per person
Slices of fresh tomato
Lots of almond mayo (page 60)
Lettuce or salad greens

Method :
Coat the salad greens in the mayo, and also spread some on the bread. Top with the other ingredients, along with some tomato sauce if you wish.

Mushroom Lentil and Barley Burgers

LF

Prepare the mixture for cabbage rolls, following the directions on page 75. Add 4-6 tablespoons of tomato sauce, 2-4 tablespoons vegan worcestershire sauce, soy-free tamari or coconut aminos, and 4 tablespoons chickpea flour. Bake for 30 minutes as larger burgers, less for smaller patties.

Lentil Burgers

A simple burger that goes really well as a burger with the lot (page 39)

Ingredients

LF

Makes 4-6 serves

2 cups dry brown lentils
water, for cooking
1/2 cup chickpea flour (besan)
1 teaspoon salt (omit if using tamari)
1/4-1/2 teaspoon cayenne pepper
1/2 teaspoon dried oregano
1/2 teaspoon dried thyme
1/2 teaspoon wakame or kelp, optional
4 tablespoons tomato sauce
5 tablespoons vegan worcestershire sauce, soy-free tamari or coconut aminos
1 small onion, grated

Method

Bring the lentils and water to the boil. Simmer until tender, about 30-40 minutes. Drain and reserve the cooking water.

Preheat the oven to 160-200c (320-390f).

Mix the dry ingredients together, breaking up any lumps. Add the sauces and onion and thoroughly mix. Stir through the lentils, evenly coating them in this mixture, mashing them up slightly, but not completely.

Shape into 4-6 burgers or small patties and bake for around 30 minutes (20 for smaller ones), until firm and browned.

Leftover tips:
The mixture stores well in the fridge for a few days. The burgers can be frozen after shaping, and baked at another time.

41

Mushroom Rissoles

Ingredients

250g (9 oz) of mushrooms
1 medium onion
2 tablespoons vegan worcestershire sauce, soy-free tamari or coconut aminos
1 1/2 cups rolled oats or gluten free breadcrumbs
1/2 cup chickpea flour (besan)
1/4 cup nutritional yeast (savoury yeast flakes)
1 teaspoon black pepper, ground
1 1/2 teaspoons salt (reduce if using tamari)
a pinch of cayenne pepper
1 1/2 cups cooked borlotti (pinto) or other beans (1 400g (14oz) tin)

Method

In a food processor, blend the mushrooms, the onion, worcestershire sauce and half the oats until it is well-blended and paste-like.

In a medium mixing bowl, squash any lumps out of the chickpea flour. Add the mushroom mixture, nutritional yeast, pepper, salt and cayenne pepper.

Blend the beans in the food processor until smoothish. Add this and the remaining 3/4 cup of oats to the mixture.

Shallow fry or bake as heaped-tablespoon sized patties.

Baking takes 30 minutes, or slightly longer if the mixture has been in the fridge. Shallow frying takes about 5 minutes for each side.

Leftover tips: The mixture stores well in the fridge for a few days.
Nightshade-free option: Omit the cayenne pepper, and make sure your worcestershire sauce is nightshade free.

Lentil Meatballs

Delicious and versatile with a subtle cheesy taste, great served with pasta or in a wrap, sandwich or salad.

OGF

Serves 2

Ingredients
1 cup dry brown lentils
water, for cooking
1/3 cup almonds or almond meal
1/3 cup oats or gluten free breadcrumbs (use quick oats or breadcrumbs if you don't have a food processor)
1/2 cup chickpea flour (besan)
1/4 cup nutritional yeast (savoury yeast flakes)
pinch of cayenne pepper
1 teaspoon salt
1 1/2 teaspoons dried oregano (1 1/2 tablespoons fresh)
1/4 teaspoon dried thyme, or 1 teaspoon fresh
3 tablespoons tomato sauce or ketchup

Method
Bring the lentils and water to the boil. Simmer for 30 minutes or until tender.

Preheat the oven to 160-200c (320-390f).

If using a food processor, grind the almonds until fine, then grind the oats. Put this in a mixing bowl with the chickpea flour, nutritional yeast, cayenne pepper, salt and herbs.

Drain the lentils and blend in a food processor (mash if you don't have one) with the tomato sauce. Add this to the other ingredients, thoroughly mix in and then shape into heaped-teaspoon sized balls.

Bake for 20-30 minutes.

Best served with caramelised onion and tomato pasta sauce (page 61).

Chickpea 'Fish' and Chips

In the days when I cooked with tofu I would often marinate it in wakame and vinegar, and serve it with chips. Using the same flavours I created these chickpea-based patties that taste even better. Best served with fresh lemon juice.

Kitchen time 10 minutes
Cooking time 30-40 minutes

LF NF OGF
(under 45 minutes)

Serves 2

Ingredients
1 recipe oven chips (page 83)

For the patties:
1/3 cup wakame (if you don't have wakame, you could substitute with ripped up sushi nori, or another sea vegetable)
1/3 cup vinegar
1-2 teaspoons barley malt syrup (optional)
1/4-1/2 teaspoon salt
1/4 cup water
2 1/4 cups cooked chickpeas (1 1/2 400g (14oz) tins)
1/2 cup flour (barley, wholemeal spelt, wholewheat or gluten free)

2/3 cup barley flour, for flouring,
or the crumbing ingredients for seitan schnitzel (page 54)

Method
Preheat the oven to 160-200c (320-390f).

Prepare the chips, following the directions on page 83, and put them in the oven once it's heated up.

In a mixing bowl, combine the wakame, vinegar, barley malt syrup, salt and water. Leave for at least 5 minutes, for the wakame to soak.

Use a fork or food processor to mash the chickpeas as finely as possible, use some of the wakame/vinegar mixture to help with this.

Add the rest of the wakame/vinegar mixture, along with the flour and combine until evenly mixed.

Take tablespoons of the mixture and shape into patties or 'fingers' and coat in flour, or crumb with the same mixtures for seitan schnitzel, page 54. Place on an oiled baking tray, and brush the tops with oil if you wish.

Once the potatoes have 20 minutes to go, (when they move around freely and are all golden on one side), put the patties in the oven and bake for 20 minutes, flipping over once towards the end of the cooking.

Alternatively, shallow fry for 5 minutes on each side, until golden.

44

Gluten-free option: Use a gluten-free flour and omit the barley malt syrup.

Felafel

Kitchen time 10-15 minutes
Soaking time 8-24 hours
Cooking time 10-25 minutes

NSI **LF option NF**

Serves 2

Making these from dried beans is tastier and cheaper than using a packet mix, with not much extra time or effort needed. Made with broad beans, they are nicer than any restaurant felafels I've eaten. Best served in flat bread with salad and tahini sauce or cashew sour cream, they're also good served as patties with oven chips.

Ingredients

1 cup dried broad beans (fava beans) or chickpeas
2 cloves of garlic
1 tiny onion
2 teaspoons ground cumin
1/2 teaspoon ground coriander
1/2 teaspoon ground black pepper
1/2 teaspoon salt
optional pinch of ground cloves, nutmeg, cinnamon, allspice, fenugreek and ginger
optional 1/4 - 1/2 cup fresh parsley, or a mix of parsley and coriander (cilantro)
optional 2 tablespoons chickpea flour (besan) mixed with 2 tablespoons water

Method

Soak the beans in cold water overnight, or for 24 hours. Drain and rinse.

Combine all ingredients except for the beans in a food processor and blend until evenly chopped. Add the beans and blend until it's very finely ground and fluffy. You may need to scrape the sides of the food processor a couple of times, to make sure it's evenly blended.

Refrigerate for at least an hour. If the mixture seems a bit crumbly, you can add 2 tablespoons of chickpea flour and 2 tablespoons of water to help it stick together.

Take tablespoons of the mixture and form them into patties, then fry in half a centimetre (1/4 inch) of hot oil until lightly browned, a couple of minutes, flip and cook the other side for a couple of minutes, until lightly browned. Alternatively, you could brush the patties with oil and bake for 20-25 minutes.

Serve with tahini sauce (page 59) or cashew sour cream (page 60).

45

Spicy Black Bean Patties

Ingredients
1 1/2 cups cooked black beans (1 400g (14oz) tin)
1 small onion, grated
2 cloves garlic, finely chopped
1/2 teaspoon salt
2 teaspoons paprika
1/8-1/4 teaspoon cayenne pepper
1 teaspoon oregano
1 teaspoon agave or maple syrup
1 teaspoon vinegar (red wine or apple cider)
optional 1 teaspoon vegan worcestershire sauce
1/3 cup cornmeal or breadcrumbs, plus extra for coating

Method
Combine all the ingredients except for the cornmeal in a mixing bowl. Mash as much as possible, then stir through the cornmeal. Leave to sit while you prepare the side dishes.

Take tablespoons of the mixture and squash into patties, coat in cornmeal, then brush with oil and bake for 20-25 minutes, or shallow fry for about 5 minutes on one side, flip, and fry for around 2 minutes on the other side, until lightly browned.

These are delicious served with cashew sour cream (page 60) or avocado mayo (page 59).

Because these patties contain nothing to replace the egg that would normally bind a burger together, they are more breakable than some of my other burger recipes. Feel free to add a chickpea flour, flaxseed or chia seed egg replacer (page 7) to the mixture to fix this.

Lentil Kofta

I like to serve these Indian spiced patties in the coconut sauce with some brown rice, but they can also be served in a sandwich, wrap, salad, or as an hors d'oeuvre with mango chutney.

LF NF option

Ingredients

1 cup dry brown lentils
water for cooking
1/4 cup chickpea flour (besan)
1/4 cup rolled oats or gluten free breadcrumbs
1 tablespoon fresh ginger, finely chopped
2 cloves garlic, finely chopped
1 tablespoon peanut butter
1/2-1 teaspoon salt
1 teaspoon garam masala
a pinch or two of cayenne pepper

Method

Serves 2-3

Bring the lentils and water to the boil, simmer until tender, about 30-40 minutes and drain, reserving 1/4 cup of the cooking water.

Preheat the oven to 160-200c (320-390f).

Mix the rest of the ingredients together, breaking up any lumps in the chickpea flour. Add the lentils and water, mashing them up as much as you can and mixing it all thoroughly.

Roll into heaped-teaspoon sized balls (having some water on your hands helps with this) and place on a lined or greased baking sheet. Bake for 20 minutes.

Coconut Sauce GF NF option (under 45 minutes)

This makes a very rich sauce for a restaurant-style curry, it can easily be made to serve 4-6 instead by doubling the water and adding some extra spices to taste. It can also be made lower in fat by only using half the can of coconut cream and some extra water.

Ingredients:

1 small to medium onion, diced
1 1/2 tablespoons fresh ginger, finely chopped
4 cloves garlic, finely chopped
2 teaspoons turmeric
1 teaspoon garam masala
1 cup water
1 400g (14oz) tin coconut cream
cayenne pepper and salt, to taste
1 teaspoon garam masala, extra
2 teaspoons lemon juice (optional)

Sauté the onion over medium-high heat until tender and fragrant, about five minutes. Add the ginger, garlic, turmeric and garam masala and stir for another 30-60 seconds. Add the water, coconut cream, cayenne pepper and salt. Bring to the boil, reduce heat and simmer for at least 2 minutes. When the koftas are cooked, add the extra garam masala and the koftas to the sauce, gently coating them in sauce. Sprinkle in a little lemon juice, if using, and serve over brown rice.

Nightshade-free option: Omit the cayenne pepper

Chickpea Salad Sandwiches

This creamy salad is very quick to make.

Ingredients

1 1/2 cups cooked chickpeas (1 400g (14oz) tin)
4-6 tablespoons almond mayonnaise (page 60)
1/2-1 teaspoon lemon juice or apple cider vinegar
1-2 sliced tomatoes, if in season, or grated carrot
As many salad greens as you want
Slices of bread, halved rolls, mountain bread or tortillas, 1-2 per serve

NSI **LF**
NF option OGF
(under 45 minutes)

Serves 2

Method

Roughly mash the chickpeas in a mixing bowl and add the mayo.
Prepare the other ingredients, dressing the salad with extra mayonnaise if you want. Spread an additional 1-2 tablespoons of mayonnaise on each slice of bread, then cover with tomatoes (or carrots), salad greens and the chickpeas.

Nightshade-free option: use carrot instead of tomato

48

SEITAN DISHES

Easy Baked Seitan

This basic seitan recipe can be used in any of the recipes in this chapter. For some variation, half a cup of mashed up beans can be added to the mixture, or the seasonings adjusted to suit whatever dish you're using this in.

Kitchen time 5-10 minutes
Resting time 15 minutes
Baking time 15-20 minutes

LF option NF option
OGF option
(under 45 minutes)

Makes 4 serves

Ingredients
Dry ingredients
1 - 1 1/4 cups gluten (vital wheat gluten)
1-2 tablespoons wholemeal wheat, barley or spelt flour
optional 1/4 cup chickpea flour (besan)
2-3 tablespoons nutritional yeast (savoury yeast flakes)
1/2 - 1 teaspoon salt (omit if using tamari or coconut aminos)
a pinch or 2 of cayenne pepper (optional)
optional 1-2 teaspoons dried herbs of your choice

Wet ingredients
2-3 tablespoons vegan worcestershire sauce, soy-free tamari or coconut aminos
(for best results) 1-2 tablespoons tahini or oil (melted coconut, olive or sunflower)
optional 1 tablespoon mustard
water - start with half a cup

Method
Preheat the oven to 160-200c (320-390f).

Mix the dry ingredients together.

In a separate measuring cup or mixing bowl, mix the wet ingredients together, adding enough water for the ingredients to measure 1 cup in total (1/2 cup to 3/4 cup).

Stir the wet ingredients into the dry mix, then knead it to combine, adding more water, a little at a time, as needed. You want for this mixture to be about the consistency of a bread dough - not too wet, but not too dry. It is better to have it on the dry side, because a wet dough will take longer to bake and the texture isn't as good.

Set this aside for at least 5 minutes. Now is a good time to prepare any of the potato or roasted vegetable side dishes from this book. See pages 82-83.

Take the portion of seitan that you wish to use immediately, and put the rest in the fridge. It will keep for up to five days.

To create texture in the seitan, stretch out the portion you are using now, and fold it in half, repeat this five to eight times. To serve as simple cutlets, shape into a rough log-like shape, and then take slices around 1-2cm (1/2-1") thick and place on an oiled baking sheet. Brush the tops with oil and when your side dish has 15 minutes to go, place the tray in the oven and bake until the bottom of the cutlets are lightly browned, about 10-12 minutes. Flip over, brushing the tops with more oil, or the 'bbq sauce' glaze from this page. Bake until the bottoms are browned, another 5 minutes or so.

Onion- and garlic-free option: check that the vegan worcestershire sauce you're using is suitable, or use coconut aminos or soy-free tamari.
Nightshade-free option: same as onion and garlic free option, and also omit the cayenne pepper from the mixture.
Leftover tips: The uncooked seitan will keep in the fridge for up to five days, and can be used in a variety of dishes in this chapter.

'BBQ Sauce' Glaze
Makes enough for 2 serves
2 teaspoons oil (toasted sesame, melted coconut, olive or sunflower)
2 teaspoons vegan worcestershire sauce
optional 1 teaspoon barley malt syrup, or other sweetener
a pinch of salt

Savoury Seitan Breakfast

This makes a great dinner or lunch

Ingredients

1/2 quantity easy baked seitan dough (page 50)
1 recipe hash browns (page 82)
1 400g (14oz) tin soy-free vegan baked beans
2-4 big leaves of kale or silverbeet (chard), stems removed, ripped into smallish pieces
Optional raw tomato, to serve

OGF option
(under 45 minutes)

Serves 2

Method

Follow the seitan recipe, and put it in the oven.

Make the hash brown recipe; start frying it when the seitan has about five minutes to go.

Heat the baked beans in a small saucepan over medium-high heat. Stir often until boiling, then reduce the heat and gently simmer until the hash browns are finished. Once the seitan and hash browns are done, add the greens to the baked beans and stir through, until brightly coloured and slightly wilted.

Onion- and garlic-free option: Follow the OGF directions for the baked seitan, and make sure the baked beans you're using are onion- and garlic-free.

'Steak' and Chips with Onion and Pepper Gravy

Ingredients

Kitchen time 20-25 minutes

Potatoes for oven chips (page 83)
1/2 quantity easy baked seitan (page 50)
2-3 onions, cut into half moons
1 tablespoon flour (barley, wholemeal spelt, or wholewheat)
1 cup water
3 tablespoons Worschestershire sauce, soy-free tamari or coconut aminos
1 tablespoon vinegar (preferably balsamic)
salt and lots of pepper to taste

NF option
(under 45 minutes)

Serves 2

Method

Preheat the oven to 160-200c (320-390f).

Make the seitan until the resting period, then prepare the chips and get them in the oven. Chop up the onion while the chips are baking, and when the chips have 20 minutes to go, divide the seitan in 2, and stretch and fold each piece 5-8 times, stretching out to make it into a 1cm (1/2") thick 'steak'. Place these on an oiled baking sheet and brush with oil. Bake for 10-15 minutes, until the bottom is browned, then flip over, brush with oil or Worcestershire sauce and bake the other side for about 5 minutes, making sure they are cooked in the middle. Alternatively you could bake these according to the 'easy baked seitan' recipe (page 50), for smaller, faster cooking 'steaks'.

As soon as the seitan is in the oven, heat the onions and 2 teaspoons of olive oil in a frying pan over medium-high heat. Stir constantly until fragrant and soft, about eight minutes, then stir through the flour for a few seconds, and add the water, vinegar and sauce. Bring to the boil while stirring, then turn the heat down to low and simmer until the seitan and chips are ready, stirring every now and then. Add salt and pepper to taste.

Serve with steamed broccoli, kale chips (page 84) or salad.

Nightshade-free option: Use swede (rutabaga) instead of potato for the chips, and follow the nightshade-free instructions in the easy baked seitan recipe (page 50).

Seitan Parmigiana

An Australian pub classic, best served with oven chips and salad.

LF option
(under 45 minutes)

Ingredients

Makes 1-4 serves

1/4 recipe easy baked seitan dough (page 50) per person
1/2 cup of flour (barley, wholemeal spelt or wholewheat)
1/2 cup of vegan milk
2/3 cup of breadcrumbs or cornmeal for breading
1/4 recipe marinara sauce per person (page 61) or use premade marinara sauce or tomato sauce
2 tablespoons cashew cheese (page 60) or cheesy lasagne sauce (page 65) per person

Method

Preheat the oven to 160-200c (320-390f)
Follow the directions on page 50 to create the seitan mix, leave to rest for at least 5 minutes.

While the seitan is resting, make the marinara sauce (page 61), leave it to simmer on the lowest setting until you are ready to use it. Make the cashew cheese (page 60) now too.

Oil a baking sheet, and divide the dough into four pieces, stretch and fold each piece that you are cooking now 5-8 times, finally stretching each one to be about 1-2cm (1/2-1") thick. Place on the tray and brush the tops with oil.

Bake for 10-15 minutes, until the bottom is browned. If you are serving this with oven chips (page 83), prepare these now and get them in the oven. Flip the seitan over and brush with oil. Bake for another 5 minutes, until the bottom is browned.

Take out of the oven, and cover each piece liberally in the flour.

When the chips have 20 minutes to go, take each floured piece of seitan and dip into the vegan milk, then cover with breadcrumbs. Return to the baking tray and bake until the bottom is browned, about 5-10 minutes. Flip over, cover each one with marinara sauce and then top with cashew cheese, and bake until the sauces are hot, about 5-10 minutes.

I like to sometimes season the breadcrumbs or cornmeal by adding a finely chopped clove of garlic, a teaspoon of nutritional yeast and 1/2 a teaspoon of kelp flakes.

Low fat option: Use 1/2 a recipe of servo-style cheesy sauce (page 76), or 1/4 recipe cheesy lasagne sauce (page 65) to top 4 parmigianas instead of cashew cheese.

Leftover tips: the seitan mix, marinara sauce and cashew cheese all keep well in the fridge for about five days, for easy meals later in the week.

Seitan Schnitzel

Ingredients
1/4 quantity easy baked seitan mixture (page 50) per person
1/2 cup chickpea flour (besan)
2/3 cup water
breadcrumbs or cornmeal for coating

LF option NF option
OGF option
(under 45 minutes)

Makes 1-4 serves

If you don't have chickpea flour, you can coat this in the same way as parmigiana (page 53).

Method
Preheat the oven to 160-200c (320-390f).

Follow the directions on page 50 to create the seitan mix, leave it to rest for at least 5 minutes.

Divide the mixture into 4, stretch and fold each piece that you are cooking with now 5-8 times, finally stretching it out to create a steak about 1cm (1/2") thick.

Brush a baking tray with oil and put the seitan steaks on it. Brush them with oil and bake until the bottom is browned, about 10-15 minutes. Flip over, brush with oil, and bake until the other side is browned, about another 5 minutes. Remove from oven.

When your side dish has 20 minutes to go, put the chickpea flour in a bowl, using a fork to break up any lumps. Add a pinch of salt, and then gradually add the water, to form a runny mixture.

Dip each piece of seitan in this mixture, making sure it is thoroughly coated. Dip into breadcrumbs, then place on an oiled baking sheet. Return to the oven and bake until the bottom is browned, about 5-10 minutes, flip over and bake for a few more minutes, until the other side is browned.

Side dish tips: Kartoffelpuffer (page 82), oven chips (page 83), spätzel (page 85), steamed broccoli, salad or crispy kale chips (page 84).

Onion- and garlic-free option, nightshade-free option and low fat options: Use the options on the easy baked seitan recipe (page 50)

Leftover tips: The seitan mixture, the baked seitan and the chickpea flour batter will keep in the fridge for a few days.

Cordon Bleu

A perfect accompaniment to spätzel (page 85) or kartoffelpuffer (page 82).

Ingredients
1/4 recipe easy baked seitan mixture (page 50) per person
2 tablespoons cashew cheese (page 60) per person
1/2 cup chickpea flour (besan)
2/3 cup water
breadcrumbs or cornmeal for coating

Makes 1-4 serves

Method
Preheat the oven to 160-200c (320-390f).

Follow the directions on page 50 to create the seitan mix, leave to rest for at least 5 minutes.

Divide the mixture into 4, stretch and fold each piece that you are cooking with now 5-8 times, finally stretching it out to create a steak about 1.5-2cm (3/4") thick.

Brush a baking tray with oil and put the seitan steaks on it. Brush them with oil and bake until the bottom is browned, about 10-15 minutes. Flip over, brush with oil, and bake until the other side is browned, about another 5 minutes. Remove from oven.

While the seitan is baking, make the cashew cheese according to the directions on page 60.

With a bread knife (or other serrated knife) carefully make a slit through the middle of each baked 'steak', like you were slicing through a bread roll. Open the 'steaks' and spread 2 tablespoons of cashew cheese on each one, sprinkling with some chopped parsley or chives if you wish.

When your side dish has 20 minutes to go, or 20 minutes before you wish to serve the cordon bleu, put the chickpea flour in a bowl, using a fork to break up any lumps. Add a pinch of salt, and then gradually add the water, to form a runny mixture.

Dip each piece of seitan in this mixture, making sure it is thoroughly coated. Dip into breadcrumbs, then place on an oiled baking sheet. Return to the oven and bake until the bottom is browned, about 10 minutes, flip over and bake for a few more minutes, until the other side is browned.

Onion- and garlic-free option, nightshade-free option: use the options on the easy baked seitan recipe (page 50)

Leftover tips: The seitan mixture, the baked seitan, the cashew cheese and the chickpea flour batter will keep in the fridge for a few days.

Nuggets

Ingredients

1/4 - 1 recipe easy baked seitan mixture (with some sage and thyme added, if you want), page 50
1/2 cup chickpea flour (besan)
2/3 cup water
a pinch of salt, 1/2 teaspoon dried sage (optional)
3/4 cup cornmeal or breadcrumbs and 1/4 cup nutritional yeast (makes enough breading for 4 serves)

Makes 1-4 serves

Method

Preheat the oven to 160-200c (320-390f).

Follow the directions on page 50 to create the seitan mix, leave to rest for 15 minutes.

If you're serving this with oven chips (page 83), get these in the oven now.

Take the portion of seitan that you plan to use now and stretch and fold it 5-8 times. Rip tablespoon-sized chunks off this, and place on a plate or bowl.

Mix the chickpea flour, salt and sage. Slowly add the water, to form a runny mixture. On a small plate, mix up the nutritional yeast and cornmeal. Dip each chunk of seitan into the chickpea flour mixture, then roll it in the cornmeal and nutritional yeast mixture. Place on an oiled baking sheet and bake until the bottom is lightly browned, about 10-15 minutes, then flip over and bake for another 5-10 minutes, until the other side is browned. Slice one in half and check that the middle is cooked, then serve.

Chinese Lemon Seitan

A healthier version of a vegetarian Chinese restaurant favourite.

Ingredients
1/2 a recipe of easy baked seitan (page 50)
Lemon sauce:
2 tablespoons flour (barley, wholemeal spelt or wholewheat)
2 tablespoons raw sugar or rapadura
2 tablespoons nutritional yeast (savoury yeast flakes)
zest of one large lemon
1/4 cup lemon juice (1-2 lemons)
1-2 tablespoons fresh ginger, finely chopped
1 clove garlic, finely chopped
1/2 a teaspoon coconut oil (optional)
1 cup water
salt, pepper and apple cider vinegar to taste

LF option NF option
(under 45 minutes)

Serves 2

Method
Preheat the oven to 160-200c (320-390f).

Make the seitan until the resting period, prepare the sauce and any side dishes while you wait.

When the seitan has finished resting, stretch and fold it 5-8 times, then rip off small chunks (about the size of 1-2 teaspoons), stretch them out, and place on an oiled baking sheet. Brush the tops with oil and bake for 10 minutes, or until the bottom is browned, flip over and bake for another couple of minutes, until the other side is browned.

While the seitan is baking, combine the sauce ingredients by first mixing the dry ingredients, and then slowly adding the water. Bring to the boil while constantly stirring. Reduce heat and add the baked seitan, stirring to coat.

Serve with barley, brown rice or noodles and some raw or lightly cooked vegetables. In the photo I have made a quick stir fry by toasting a tablespoon of sesame seeds, adding a teaspoon of oil and a small onion, cut into wedges, and stir frying until it browns, then I have added half a julienned carrot and a small head of broccoli, cut into small florets and stir fried for another couple of minutes, until just cooked.

Nightshade-free option, low fat option: Follow the nightshade-free option/low fat option instructions for the baked seitan.

SAVOURY SAUCES

AND OTHER HOMEMADE CONDIMENTS

Avocado Mayo

Ingredients
1/4-1/2 a ripe avocado
1-2 teaspoons apple cider vinegar
vegan milk
1-2 teaspoons olive oil
salt and pepper, to taste

Method
Thoroughly mash the avocado, making sure there are no chunks left. Slowly mix in the vinegar and milk, until it is about as thin as you would like the mayo to be. Drizzle in the oil while stirring, continuing to stir until it is mixed in. Season with salt and pepper and serve right away.

Gluten-free option: Make sure to use a gluten free vegan milk.

Peanut sauce

Ingredients
1/2 cup peanut butter
1/2 cup water
1 teaspoon barley malt syrup (optional)
1 teaspoon apple cider vinegar
salt, to taste
optional 2 cloves garlic, finely chopped

Method
Whisk all the ingredients together until combined.

Gluten-free option: Omit the barley malt syrup, or replace it with another sweetener.

Tahini sauce

Ingredients
1/3 cup tahini
1-3 cloves of garlic, finely chopped
optional handful of parsley, finely chopped
a pinch of salt
a pinch of ground cumin
1/6 cup lemon juice or apple cider vinegar
1/6 cup water
1 tablespoon olive oil

Method
Put the tahini, garlic, parsley, salt and cumin in a bowl, slowly add the lemon juice and water, whisking with a fork to combine. Don't worry if it doesn't mix well straight away, more whisking will do the trick. Whisk through the oil and serve.

Sweet Mustard Sauce or Salad Dressing

Ingredients
3 teaspoons olive oil, or 1 teaspoon oil and 2 teaspoons water
1 teaspoon agave or maple syrup
1 teaspoon apple cider vinegar
1 teaspoon dijon, or other smooth mustard

Method: Whisk all ingredients together with a fork and serve. For a lower fat sauce, you can replace some or all of the oil with water.

Salad Dressings

GF NSI **LF option** NF OGF   Kitchen time 5 minutes
(under 45 minutes)

Each of these recipes makes enough to coat a two serve side salad. The method is the same for all of them: Whisking the ingredients together until smooth.

Sweet and Sour Tahini Dressing
1 tablespoon tahini
1 tablespoon liquid from picked gherkins, or any other pickled vegetable

Vinaigrette
3 teaspoons olive oil
1 teaspoon vinegar (balsamic, apple cider, red wine, white wine)
optional 1/2 - 1 teaspoon dijon mustard

Sweet Apple Cider Dressing
3 teaspoons water
1 teaspoon apple cider vinegar
1 teaspoon apple juice concentrate, agave, or other honey replacer

Almond Mayonnaise

GF NSI **NF** OGF   Kitchen time 5 minutes
(under 45 minutes)

Ingredients:
1 cup almonds
1 cup water
zest of half a lemon
3 teaspoons lemon juice
apple cider vinegar, to taste (around 3 to 6 teaspoons)
salt and pepper, to taste (around 1/2 to 1 teaspoon of each)
1/2 cup vegan milk
1/4 cup olive oil

Method:
For best results, soak the almonds for as long as you have the patience (up to 24 hours), but a few minutes is fine also.

60   In a blender combine half the water and all the almonds. Blend until smooth. Add the rest of the water, along with the lemon zest, juice, vinegar, salt, pepper and vegan milk. Blend until smooth and combined. Slowly drizzle in the olive oil while blending.

Cashew Cheese

GF **NF** OGF   Kitchen time 3 minutes
(under 45 minutes)

This makes a thick cheesy spread that's perfect for spreading on bread for burgers with the lot (page 39), making a quick meal of grilled cheese and kale on toast, and for use in recipes such as Parmigiana (page 53), Cheezeburger (page 40) and Cordon Bleu (page 55).

Ingredients:
3/4 cup cashews, sunflower seeds or almonds
1/2 cup water
1/2 cup nutritional yeast (savoury yeast flakes)
1 teaspoon apple cider vinegar
optional 1 teaspoon agave or sugar
1/2 teaspoon salt

Method:
For best results, soak the cashews in the water before blending for as little as a few minutes or as long as 24 hours.

In a blender or food processor, combine all the ingredients on a low setting. Increase the speed to the highest setting after 20 seconds then blend for another 2 minutes or so, until smooth. This will thicken in the fridge.

Cashew Sour Cream

Kitchen time 3 minutes   GF NSI **NF** OGF
(under 45 minutes)

Ingredients:
1 cup cashews or sunflower seeds
1 cup water
3/4 teaspoon salt
1/2 teaspoon sugar (optional)
3-6 teaspoons apple cider vinegar

Method:
Combine all the ingredients in a blender, and blend until smooth. For best results soak the cashews for at least a few minutes before blending.

Marinara sauce

This is my basic Italian tomato sauce recipe, for use with Parmigiana (page 53) and Red Lentil Bolognese (page 33). Almost as simple as opening a jar of premade stuff, but much tastier and cheaper.

NSI **LF** (under 45 minutes)

Ingredients

1 onion, diced
2-4 cloves garlic, finely chopped
400g (14oz) diced tomatoes (1 tin)
1/3 - 1/2 a cup water or red wine
2 teaspoons vinegar (red wine or apple cider)
pinch of two of cayenne pepper
1 teaspoon dried oregano
a pinch of dried thyme
salt, to taste.

Method

Sauté the onion over medium-high heat until fragrant and soft, about 5 minutes. Stir through the garlic for about a minute, then add the rest of the ingredients and bring to the boil. Simmer for at least 5 minutes, or as long as you want.

Caramelised Onion and Tomato Pasta Sauce

This is a really nice sauce to use with lentil meatballs, page 43, it can also be used in any recipe that calls for marinara sauce.

Kitchen time 10-15 minutes

NSI **LF** (under 45 minutes)

Ingredients

1 huge onion, or 2 medium ones, cut into half or quarter moons
400g (14oz) diced tomatoes (1 tin)
1/3 cup wine or water
1 teaspoon vinegar (red wine, balsamic or apple cider)
1/2 teaspoon dried oregano (2 teaspoons fresh)
pinch of cayenne pepper
salt, to taste

Method

If you're making this to serve with lentil meatballs (page 43) start making it as soon as the lentil meatballs are in the oven.

Heat a little oil in a frying pan on medium high heat. When it is hot, add the onion. Stir constantly for 5-10 minutes, until soft and caramel coloured. Add the rest of the ingredients, bring to the boil, then gently simmer for as long as you want, adding more water if it dries out.

Shepherds Pie

A hearty and healthy pie that's perfect for cold weather.

NSI **LF NF option**)

Makes 3-4 serves

Ingredients
2/3 cup dry brown lentils
1/3 cup barley
4 medium potatoes (around 650g/1.4lb), chopped into chunks
1 medium onion, finely chopped
1 medium carrot, diced
1 1/2 tablespoons flour (barley, wholemeal spelt, wholewheat or gluten free)
1 tablespoon vegan worcestershire sauce, coconut aminos or soy-free tamari
dried herbs of your choice (I use 1 teaspoon rosemary, 1 teaspoon thyme and 1/2 teaspoon oregano)
optional 1 teaspoon barley malt syrup
1 teaspoon vinegar (malt or apple cider)
3/4 cup peas, or cooked beans of your choice
optional 1 tablespoon fresh parsley
3-4 big leaves kale or silverbeet, ripped into small pieces
Salt and pepper, to taste
Vegan milk, salt and pepper, for mashing potatoes

Method
Bring the lentils and barley to the boil in a pot with at least 4 cups of water. Simmer for 30 minutes, or until the lentils are tender. Drain, reserving 1 - 1 1/2 cups of the cooking water.

Bring a big pot of water to the boil for the potatoes. Add the potatoes and bring to the boil. Reduce heat and cook on a medium heat for 20 minutes, until mashable.

Preheat the oven to 160-200c (320-390f).

In a large pan, sauté the onion until tender and fragrant. Add the carrot and stir for another minute. Stir through the flour, then slowly add the lentil and barley cooking water, stirring while it thickens.

Add the worcestershire sauce, dried herbs, barley malt, vinegar, peas, lentils and barley and stir through. Bring to the boil while stirring, reduce heat and simmer for 5 minutes. Stir through the fresh parsley and kale. Adjust seasonings with salt and pepper and take off the heat.

Mash the potatoes with some vegan milk until it gets to a good consistency, add a little olive oil if you want a richer mash, or some garlic for extra flavour. Adjust the seasonings with salt and pepper.

To assemble, place the lentil and barley mixture in a 20cm (8") square or round dish, or in separate bowls. Top with the mash and place in the oven until the filling is bubbly and the mash is crispy, around 20-30 minutes. For a faster meal you could just place it under the grill (broiler) instead.

Gluten-free option: Use rice instead of barley, omit the barley malt syrup and make sure your worcestershire sauce and vegan milk are gluten-free.

Nightshade-free option: Use swede (rutabaga) or celeriac instead of potato. Make sure your worcestershire sauce is nightshade-free.

Leftover tips: The mixtures and the prepared pies will keep in the fridge for a few days, or in the freezer for a few months.

Lentil and Mushroom Pie

Kitchen time 20 minutes
Total time 40-70 minutes

NSI
LF option NF
(under 45 minutes option)

Makes 4 serves

A savoury and hearty one-crust pie that can either be baked without the filling, for a meal in under 45 minutes, or baked as pot pies.
For a two-crust pie, double the pastry recipe.

Ingredients
2 cups dry brown lentils
water, for cooking

For the pastry:
1 1/2 cups wholemeal wheat or gluten free flour
1 cup barley, wholemeal spelt, wholemeal wheat or gluten free flour
1/4 teaspoon salt
1/2 cup oil (melted coconut, olive or sunflower)
1/4-1/2 cup cold water, as needed

2 medium onions, cut into half moons
250g (8.8oz) mushrooms, sliced (1 heaped dinner plate, after slicing)
1/2 cup vegan red wine (or cooking water plus 1 tablespoon red wine vinegar)
salt, to taste
optional pinch of kelp
cracked pepper, to taste
4-5 medium leaves kale or silverbeet (chard), ripped into small pieces
optional 2 tablespoons savoury yeast flakes

Method
Bring the lentils and water to the boil, reduce the heat and simmer for 30-40 minutes, until the lentils are tender.

Preheat the oven to 160-200c (320-390f).

Prepare the pastry by mixing the flours and the salt together. Stir through the oil and then crumble with your fingers until it is evenly mixed in. Add the water, a little at a time, until the dough sticks together without easily crumbling apart. Refrigerate while you prepare the rest of the recipe. If you wish to make this as an under 45 minute meal, bake the pastry now by pressing it into a pie plate or springform pan and baking it for 10-20 minutes, until golden. Keep it warm in the oven while you prepare the filling.

When the lentils have cooked, sauté the onion over medium heat until tender and fragrant. Add the mushrooms and sauté for a few more minutes, until they start to break down and change the colour of the onions. Add the red wine or water, salt, kelp, pepper, lentils and kale and bring to the boil. Reduce heat and simmer for 2 minutes or more. You may have to add a little more water.

Place the filling in individual bowls or a lasagne dish and top with the pastry and bake for 20 minutes, until the pastry is cooked.

Serve with a red wine reduction and some truffle oil, if you want to impress guests, or some tomato sauce for an Aussie chip shop taste.

64 **Low fat option:** Cook and mash potatoes according to the directions for shepherds pie (page 63) and use this to top the pies with.

Lentil Lasagne

This recipe makes two 20cm (8 inch) square lasagnes consisting of three layers of tomato and lentil mix, three layers of pasta, and one top layer of cheesy sauce. Each of these makes either two big serves alone or with salad, or can serve three to four with some heartier side dishes such as garlic bread.

Ingredients

2 cups dry split red lentils (or dry brown lentils)
5-6 cups water, for cooking
2 medium onions, diced
5-6 cloves garlic, finely chopped (optional)
2 medium carrots or zucchini, or one of each, diced
2-3 teaspoons dried herbs (e.g. oregano and thyme)
1 teaspoon salt
1 tablespoon vinegar (red wine, apple cider or balsamic)
400g-800g (14-28oz) diced tomatoes (1-2 tins)
1/3 cup red wine or lentil cooking water, plus 1 cup extra water if using only 1 tin of tomatoes
optional 4-6 big leaves of kale or silverbeet (chard), finely chopped or ripped

For the white sauce:
1/2 cup flour (whole barley, spelt, wheat or gluten free)
3/4 cup nutritional yeast (savoury yeast flakes)
1 1/2 teaspoons salt, or to taste
2 1/2 - 3 cups vegan milk
1 tablespoon olive, coconut or sunflower oil (optional)

wholemeal lasagne sheets, mountain bread or tortillas
sesame seeds, optional, for sprinkling on top

Method

Bring the lentils and water to the boil, simmer for 10 minutes (or 30 minutes, for brown lentils) and drain, reserving the cooking water.

Preheat the oven to 160-200c (320-390f).

In a large skillet or saucepan over medium-high heat, sauté the onions until tender and fragrant. Add the garlic if using, along with the carrots or zucchini, and stir for another minute or two. Add the herbs, salt, vinegar, wine or cooking water, tomatoes and lentils, and bring to the boil. Stir through the greens, if using. Reduce heat and simmer while you prepare the white sauce.

To prepare the white sauce, mix all the dry ingredients together in a medium saucepan. Mix the vegan milk in, a little at a time, to avoid lumps. Place on medium heat and continue to stir, adding the rest of the milk if there's some left, along with the oil, if using. Bring to the boil while stirring, reduce heat and simmer for two minutes, stirring,

Layer the lasagne by placing a thin layer of the tomato and lentil mixture, then a layer of pasta, repeat for another two layers of each, then top with the white sauce, sprinkle with sesame seeds, and bake for 20 minutes (40 minutes if cooking one that's been refrigerated.)

Gluten-free option: Use thinly sliced zucchini, cooked potato or sweet potato instead of the lasagne sheets.

Leftover tips: A layered lasagne ready for baking will keep in the fridge for a few days, or the freezer for a few months. The mixtures will also keep separately for a few days in the fridge.

Moussaka

Ingredients

1 1/3 cups dry brown lentils
1/2 cup barley (use brown rice for gluten-free option)
Water for cooking
1 large eggplant
2 medium onions, diced
3-5 cloves of garlic, finely chopped
400g (14oz) diced tomatoes
1 teaspoon nutmeg
2 teaspoons dried oregano
1 tablespoon vinegar (red wine or apple cider)
salt, to taste

1/4 cup olive oil, or extra vegan milk
1 teaspoon salt
1 teaspoon nutmeg
3/4 cup flour (whole barley, spelt, wheat or GF)
3 cups vegan milk

GF option NSI LF option

Makes 4-6 serves

Method

In a covered saucepan, bring the lentils, barley and water to the boil, simmer for half an hour. Drain, reserving the cooking water.

While the lentils and barley are cooking, cut the eggplant into slices, sprinkle with salt and leave for at least fifteen minutes. Rinse, squeeze out excess water and dice.

Preheat the oven to 160-200c (320-390f).

In a large frying pan on medium-high heat, sauté the onion until soft, about 2-5 minutes. Add the garlic and eggplant and stir for a couple more minutes, then reduce the heat to medium-low and continue stirring, until the eggplant is tender (about five minutes).

Add the tomatoes, nutmeg, oregano, vinegar, salt, lentils and barley. Add some of the reserved cooking water to make a thick sauce. Bring to the boil, reduce heat and simmer for 5-10 minutes, while making the white sauce.

To make the white sauce, mix the dry ingredients together, then slowly add the oil (if using) and vegan milk, a little at a time so that no lumps form. Place over medium heat and continue to stir, slowly adding the rest of the vegan milk. Continue stirring until thick and bubbly.

Assemble in a lasagne pan or casserole dish by placing a thick layer of the eggplant mixture, followed by a topping of the white sauce. Top with sesame seeds or breadcrumbs and bake for 20-40 minutes, until the top is golden.

Gluten-free option: Use lentils or brown rice instead of the barley.

Low fat option: Replace the oil in the white sauce with extra vegan milk.

Leftover tips: The assembled moussaka will keep in the fridge for a few days, or freezer for a few months. The separate mixtures will keep in the fridge for a few days.

Cannelloni with White Bean and Kale Pesto

A very impressive dish that's full of flavour and fairly quick to make.

Kitchen time 20-30 minutes
Cooking time 20-30 minutes

GF option LF (under 45 minutes)

Makes 4 serves (2 rolls per serve)

Ingredients

Pasta:
2 cups wholewheat or wholemeal semolina flour
1/2 cup chickpea flour (besan)
3/4 teaspoon salt
1 cup water

1 double recipe of marinara sauce (page 61)

Filling:
1/4 cup cashews
3 cloves garlic
2 tablespoons nutritional yeast (savoury yeast flakes)
1/2 teaspoon salt
1 teaspoon cracked pepper
1 tablespoon fresh oregano (1 teaspoon dried)
1 teaspoon lemon zest
1 tablespoon lemon juice
4 cups kale or other leafy green, ripped into small pieces
4 1/2 cups cooked cannellini or other white beans (3 400g (14oz tins)
optional 8 kalamata olives, chopped

Method

Prepare the pasta dough by mixing all the dry ingredients together, breaking up any lumps. Stir through the water and knead until evenly mixed. Set aside for at least 15 minutes.

Preheat the oven to 160-200c (320-390f).

Prepare the marinara sauce according to the directions on page 61, adding an extra 1/3 cup of water. Leave it to simmer on a very low heat while you prepare the filling.

To prepare the filling, grind the cashews, garlic, yeast, salt, pepper, oregano and lemon zest in a food processor until it reaches a pesto-like consistency. Add the lemon juice, kale, and 1/3 of the beans, continue to blend until the kale is chopped into small pieces. Mash or blend through the remaining beans.

To assemble, first place a small layer of sauce on the bottom of your baking dish. To bake half the batch, to serve two, use a 20cm (8") square lasagne dish, to bake it all at once, use a 20 x 30 cm (8"x12") dish.

Take 1/4 of the pasta dough and roll it out, flouring both sides, until it is around a 20cm (8") square. Slice into two rectangles, and place 2 tablespoons of the filling in a strip in the middle of each rectangle, topping with some chopped olives if you wish. Roll up and gently place seam side down in the baking dish. Repeat this for the other serves, then top with the remaining sauce.

Bake for 20-30 minutes.

Leftover tips: I use this to make two meals for two by making the separate mixtures (dough, sauce and filling), and using half of them the first night, then assembling and baking the other half within a few days. The entire dish can also be prepared in advance and refrigerated for a few days, or frozen for a few months.
Gluten-free option: Use a gluten-free flour blend instead of the wheat flour.

Party Pies

Ingredients
1/2 cup barley
1/2 cup dry brown lentils
water for cooking
1 medium-large onion, diced
2 tablespoons vegan worcestershire sauce, soy-free tamari or coconut aminos
1/2 a tablespoon apple cider vinegar
3 tablespoons tomato sauce or ketchup
salt, to taste
optional 1-2 cups finely chopped kale or silverbeet (chard)
6-8 sheets mountain bread, or 2 sheets soy-free vegan puff pastry

Method
Bring the barley, lentils and water to the boil. Simmer for 30 minutes, until tender but not mushy. Leave for 5-10 minutes, then drain, reserving some of the water.

Preheat the oven to 160-200c (320-390f).

Bring the pastry out of the freezer, if using.

Once the barley and lentils have finished cooking, sauté the onion over medium-high heat until soft and fragrant. Add the lentils and barley, worcestershire sauce, vinegar, tomato sauce and kale (if using), along with enough of the reserved cooking water to make a very thick gravy coating the ingredients, but not too much!

Mountain bread instructions:
To make triangle shaped pies with mountain bread, brush a sheet with water and cut in half, to make two rectangles. Put a triangle of filling towards one corner, leaving another corner that can be folded over this, along with a 1cm (1/2") edge on the other side, to be folded up. Fold the corner over the filling, then fold the edge up. Fold this triangle onto the rest of the bread, and fold the other pieces up to cover it. Larger or smaller pies could be made this way as well.

Pastry instructions:
When the pastry is thoroughly defrosted, stretch it out to make it as rectangular as possible without breaking. Cut each sheet into six rectangles, stretch each one out as much as possible, before placing it in a large muffin cup. Put approximately 2 tablespoons of the mixture in each, then fold the four corners over the mixture.

Bake for 20-30 minutes.

Gluten-free option: Use gluten free mountain bread or pastry.

Low fat option: Use mountain bread.

Leftover tips: The mixture will keep in the fridge for a few days, and the prepared pies can be frozen for a few months.

Not-Sausage Rolls

Kitchen time 5-10 minutes
Resting time 6-20 hours
Baking time 45- 60 minutes

NSI **LF option**

Makes 6-8 serves

Ingredients

1 cup dry brown lentils
4 cups water, for cooking
3 tablespoons tahini or peanut butter
4 tablespoons vegan worcestershire sauce, coconut aminos or soy-free tamari
4 tablespoons tomato sauce or ketchup
1 medium onion, grated
1 medium apple, grated
1/4 teaspoon cayenne pepper
1/2 teaspoon salt (omit if using tamari)
2-4 teaspoons dried herbs of your choice (e.g. oregano, thyme, sage)
1 cup rolled oats
4 teaspoons sesame seeds, for sprinkling (optional)
6 sheets mountain bread or 3-4 sheets soy-free vegan puff pastry

Method

Bring the lentils and water to the boil, simmer for 30 minutes then drain, reserving 1/4 cup of the cooking water.

Mix all the other ingredients together, adding the oats and water last. This mixture is easier to roll once it's been sitting for a while in the fridge, but can be made right away (it will just be a little messier).

Preheat the oven to 160-200c (320-390f).

Mountain bread instructions: Place 1/6 of the mixture in each mountain bread sheet that you are cooking with now, in a 'sausage' shape. Brush the rest of the sheet with water and roll up. Sprinkle with sesame seeds and carefully slice into smaller rolls.

Pastry instructions: Cut each pastry sheet in half, rectangularly. Place 1/6 or 1/8 of the mixture in a 'sausage' shape in the middle 1/3 of each rectangle. Roll up and seal, sprinkle with sesame seeds, then cut into smaller rolls.

Bake the rolls at 160-200c (320-390f) for half an hour.

Low fat option: Use mountain bread.

Leftover tips: The sausage roll mixture keeps in the fridge for a few days, for fast meals later on, the prepared rolls can be frozen for a few months. Baked rolls can be kept in the fridge and reheated, wrapped in foil for about half an hour.

Baked Potatoes with Hummus, Beans and Salad

Rather than including a plain recipe for hummus, I have instead included my favourite way to use hummus in a main course. The hummus from this can, of course, be made separately and served as a spread or dip. The potatoes also make a nice meal with a heated can of vegan refried beans instead of the hummus and beans. While it takes time to bake the potatoes, the rest of the recipe comes together really quickly.

Kitchen time 5-10 minutes
Cooking time 45-120 minutes

NSI **LF NF option**
OGF option

Makes 2 serves,
plus extra hummus

Ingredients
Enough potatoes for two serves

Hummus ingredients:
1/3 cup tahini
1/6 cup lemon juice or apple cider vinegar
1/6 cup water
1 clove garlic, optional
salt, to taste (about 1/2-1 teaspoon)
1 teaspoon cumin
optional cayenne pepper, to taste
optional 1 teaspoon paprika
1 1/2 cups cooked chickpeas (1 400g (14oz) tin)

1 400g (14oz) tin four bean mix, or any other kind of beans
Salad ingredients for two (Mesclun mix, lettuce, grated carrot etc)

Method
Wash the potatoes and prick them with a fork several times. Place them in a hot oven, 170-210c (340-410f) and bake until thoroughly cooked. The cooking time will depend on the size of the potatoes, and takes anywhere between 45 minutes and 120 minutes.

To make the hummus, combine the tahini, lemon juice and garlic in a food processor. Blend until combined and creamy, then mix in the salt, cumin, cayenne pepper and paprika. Add the chickpeas and blend until combined. This makes a very thick hummus, and may need to be stirred a couple of times to get the chickpeas to blend in.

If you're after a hummus with more of a restaurant-style texture, don't use all the chickpeas, only add about 3/4 of them to the mixture, and drizzle in some olive oil. You could also omit the paprika and sprinkle it on top instead, along with some finely chopped fresh parsley if you have it.

To serve this as a dish, cut crosses halfway through the potatoes and fold each corner out, mash it slightly, top with some hummus, then cover with beans and salad. You will probably have enough leftover hummus for another two serves of this dish.

70 **Onion- and garlic-free option:** Omit the garlic from the hummus.
Nightshade-free option: Use swedes (rutabagas) instead of potatoes; omit the cayenne pepper and paprika from the hummus.

Penne Pasta Bake (Baked Ziti)

Ingredients

water, for boiling
2/3 cup dry split red lentils
200-400g (7-14 oz) wholemeal penne or ziti
1-2 cups finely chopped greens or broccoli

1 recipe marinara sauce (page 61)

For the cashew or sunflower ricotta:
3/4 - 1 cup cashews or sunflower seeds
1/2 - 2/3 cup water
2-3 teaspoons lemon juice or apple cider vinegar
salt, to taste
optional 2 teaspoons nutritional yeast (savoury yeast flakes)

Optional crunchy topping:
2/3 cup breadcrumbs or cornmeal
1/4 cup nutritional yeast (savoury yeast flakes)
1-2 pinches salt
2 teaspoons olive oil or water

Method

Preheat the oven to 160-200c (320-390f).

Bring a big pot of water to the boil. Add the lentils and the pasta, boil until the pasta is tender but not mushy, about 11-13 minutes. Quickly stir through the greens or broccoli at the end of the cooking and drain.

While the pasta is boiling, make the marinara sauce according to the directions on page 61. Mix the pasta, lentils and the marinara sauce together.

Combine the cashew or sunflower ricotta ingredients in a high speed blender and blend until creamy.

Assemble this in a casserole or lasagne dish by either placing all of the pasta/marinara mixture in one layer, with the ricotta on top, or layered with a middle layer of the ricotta.

To make the optional breadcrumb mixture, just mix all the dry ingredients together and mix the oil or water in as much as you can, and sprinkle over the dish.

Bake for 15-20 minutes.

Gluten-free option: Use gluten free pasta and cornmeal instead of breadcrumbs.

Leftover tips: This can be made ahead of time and stored in the fridge or freezer until you need to bake it, but will take a bit longer to bake.

Pumpkin and Penne Pasta Bake

Ingredients

NSI option
LF option (under 45 minutes)

Serves 2-4

Water, for boiling
Half a small butternut pumpkin (350g (12.3 oz), peeled and chopped into chunks
2/3 cup dry split red lentils
200-400g (7-14 oz) wholemeal penne
1-2 cups finely chopped greens or broccoli
1 recipe marinara sauce (page 61)
2 cloves garlic
1/2 cup sunflower seeds (optional)
1/2 cup water
salt, to taste

Method

Preheat the oven to 160-200c (320-390f).

Bring a large pot of water to the boil. Add the pumpkin, lentils and pasta and bring to the boil. Cook until the pasta is tender but not mushy, about 11-13 minutes. Stir through the greens (if using) and drain.

While the pasta is boiling, prepare the marinara sauce according to the directions on page 61.

If you have a blender or food processor, blend garlic, sunflower seeds, water, salt and cooked pumpkin until smooth.

If you don't have a blender, or wish to make the recipe lower in fat, then mash the pumpkin with some of the cooking water, salt and finely chopped garlic until smooth-ish.

Mix the pasta, lentils, greens and the marinara sauce together. Place in a casserole or lasagne dish, top with the pumpkin mixture and bake for 15-30 minutes.

Gluten-free: Use gluten-free pasta.
Low fat: Follow the directions for the pumpkin topping without a blender.
Leftover tips: This can be assembled ahead of time and stored in the fridge or freezer until baking, but it will take a bit longer to bake this way.

Potato and Lentil Bake with Garlic and Cumin

Ingredients

1 cup dry brown lentils
water, for cooking
1 medium onion, diced
3 cloves of garlic, finely chopped
4 teaspoons cumin
salt, to taste
a pinch of cayenne pepper
500g (14oz) potatoes (2 big ones), finely sliced
extra finely chopped garlic, optional
5 Tablespoons sesame seeds
1 tablespoon olive oil, optional

Method

Bring the lentils and water to the boil, covered, then simmer for 30 minutes. Drain, reserving some of the cooking water.

Preheat the oven to 160-200c (320-390f).

Sauté the onion for a couple of minutes until tender and fragrant, add the garlic and stir for a minute more. Add the lentils, cumin, salt and cayenne pepper, and as much of the reserved lentil cooking water as you need to make it so that there is plenty of sauce around the lentils, but not too much, 3/4 cup is a good amount. Take off the heat.

Brush a 30cm by 20cm (11.8x7.8 inch) lasagne pan with oil and layer some potatoes on this, covering the entire base. Sprinkle with garlic if you want, then layer half the lentil mixture on top. Put another potato layer on top of this, then another layer of lentils, then finish with a third layer of potatoes. Pour a tablespoon of olive oil over the top if you wish, as evenly as you can, and sprinkle with sesame seeds.

Bake for 50-60 minutes, until the potatoes are cooked.

Nightshade-free option: Use swedes (rutabaga), parsnips or sweet potato instead of the potatoes. Omit the cayenne pepper.

Steamed Beetroot and Lentil Haggis

Kitchen time 30-40 minutes
Baking time 30-45 minutes

Ingredients

NF option

Makes 4-6 serves

1 cup dry brown lentils
water for cooking
1 1/2 cups rolled oats
1 medium onion, finely diced
1 medium to large beetroot (250g (8.8oz) finely diced
1 cup walnuts, finely chopped
1 teaspoon salt
2 tablespoons nutritional yeast (savoury yeast flakes)
1/2 teaspoon dried thyme, or 1 teaspoon fresh
1/2 teaspoon dried sage
1/2 teaspoon nutmeg
a pinch of cayenne pepper
1 tablespoon apple cider vinegar
3 tablespoons vegan worcestershire sauce, coconut aminos or soy-free tamari
optional 1 tablespoon whisky

Method

Bring the lentils and water to the boil, simmer for 30 minutes, drain and reserve 3/4 cup of the cooking water.

Preheat the oven to 160-200c (320-390f)

Toast the oats in a dry frying pan over a medium-low heat, adding a teaspoon of coconut oil if you wish, stirring occasionally for about five minutes.

Sauté the onion and beetroot for a couple of minutes on a medium-high heat. Reduce the heat to medium-low, stirring every now and then, for another 15 minutes.

Mix all the ingredients together and place in individual ramekins, oven-proof tea cups or bowls. Place these in a roasting pan 1/2 full of hot water. Cover with foil and bake for 30-45 minutes.

For haggis burgers, add 2/3 cup chickpea flour and 2/3 cup water to the mixture to make four huge or six medium burgers. Bake for 30-40 minutes.

Nightshade-free option: Omit the cayenne pepper, and check that your worcestershire sauce is nightshade-free.

Leftover tips: I like to make the oven-steamed version one night (to serve two), using half the recipe, and then make burgers the next night by adding the 1/3 cup chickpea flour and 1/3 cup water to the mixture.

Cabbage Rolls with Mushrooms, Lentils and Barley

Kitchen time 15-20 minutes
Total cooking time 50-60 minutes

LF NF option

Makes 4 serves (3 rolls per serve)

Ingredients

1 cup barley
1 1/2 cups dry brown lentils
water, for cooking
1 large onion, diced
optional 5 cloves garlic, finely chopped
2 cups finely chopped mushrooms
1 tablespoon nutritional yeast (savoury yeast flakes)
vegan worcestershire sauce, coconut aminos or soy-free tamari, to taste
salt, pepper and apple cider vinegar to taste
12 whole leaves of cabbage
paprika, for sprinkling

Method

Bring the barley, lentils and water to the boil. Reduce heat and simmer for 30 minutes. Drain and reserve the cooking water.

Preheat the oven to 160-200c (320-390f).

Sauté the onion over medium-high heat until tender and fragrant. Add the garlic and mushrooms and continue to sauté for a couple more minutes. Reduce heat and sauté for a couple more minutes until the mushrooms are tender. Add the lentils, barley and enough of the cooking water to form a thick sauce. Adjust the seasonings with nutritional yeast, worcestershire sauce, salt, pepper and vinegar.

Place about two heaped wooden spoons of this mixture in the thick end of each cabbage leaf. Roll towards the thin end, tucking the edges in if you want. The leaves may break in places if you're using raw ones; you could steam them before adding the mixture if you want, making them easier to roll.

Place each cabbage leaf in a 20x30cm (7.8 x 11.8 in) lasagne dish, one of these will fit 6 rolls. Once all the leaves are in the dish, fill this about 1/3 of the way up with water, sprinkle the rolls with paprika and cover with foil. Bake for around 20-30 minutes, until the leaves are tender.

These are delicious served with peanut sauce (page 59).

Gluten-free option: Use brown rice instead of barley.

Nightshade-free option: Check that your worcestershire sauce is nightshade-free, omit the paprika

Leftover tips: If making this as two meals for two, the second meal's portion can be made into burgers by adding 2-3 tablespoons tomato sauce, 1-2 tablespoons worcestershire sauce and 2 tablespoons chickpea flour. Bake for 30 minutes as large burgers, less time for smaller patties.

5 Minute Nacho Toppings

NSI option
LF option (under 45 minutes)

For a lower fat version of nachos, try replacing some or all of the corn chips with slices of boiled potato, zucchini, prepared polenta or ripped up mountain bread. The refried beans and salsa can be made (and the nachos assembled) while waiting for the oven to preheat. The cheesy sauce is best made while the nachos are baking, and poured over right before serving.

Serves 2

Refried Beans
1 1/2 cups cooked red kidney, borlotti, pinto or black beans (1 400g (14oz) tin)
1-2 cloves garlic
1/2 a tomato, finely chopped (or a couple of tablespoons canned tomatoes)
a pinch of two of cayenne pepper
1/2 teaspoon salt
1 teaspoon paprika
water or tomato juice, to change the consistency.

Mash the beans with your hands or a fork. Add the rest of the ingredients, adding a little liquid at a time, to get it to whatever consistency you want. When I make this with canned tomatoes, I strain them and use the juice and some of the tomatoes in this, and the rest of the tomatoes in the salsa.

Salsa
1 small onion, finely diced
1 1/2 - 2 tomatoes, finely diced (or most of the tomatoes from a 400g (14oz) tin)
optional red capsicum, if in season, finely chopped
fresh herbs of your choice, optional
pinch or two of cayenne pepper
2 teaspoons vinegar (red wine or apple cider)

Mix all these ingredients together, making sure to break up the chunks of onion into smaller pieces.

Assemble the nachos by having a layer of corn chips, boiled potatoes, zucchini or polenta, then covering this with the refried beans. Dot the salsa on top of this, then cover with corn chips. Bake for 10-20 minutes, until the beans and salsa are heated through.

Servo-Style Cheesy Sauce
5 tablespoons nutritional yeast (savoury yeast flakes)
2 tablespoons whole barley, wheat, spelt or gluten-free flour
salt, to taste
1/2 teaspoon apple cider vinegar
1-2 teaspoons raw sugar or rapadura
pinch of cayenne pepper
1/2 teaspoon kelp flakes, optional
1 cup vegan milk
1 tablespoon oil, optional (coconut, olive or sunflower)
zest of 1/4 a lemon
2 teaspoons lemon juice or apple cider vinegar

Combine the dry ingredients in a small saucepan and slowly add the milk, stirring after each addition to make sure that there are no lumps. Add the coconut oil and put on a medium heat, constantly stirring to bring it to the boil. Turn down the heat to low and continue stirring for another minute or two, until thick and bubbly. Add the lemon zest and juice, and pour over the nachos once they've finished baking.

Refried Bean Enchiladas with Cheesy Sauce

Kitchen time 15 minutes
Baking time 30 minutes

LF (under 45 minutes)
Serves 2

Ingredients

Bean filling:

3 cups cooked red kidney, borlotti (pinto) or black beans, mashed (2 400g (14oz) tins)
1 teaspoon salt
2 cloves of garlic, finely chopped
pinch or two of cayenne pepper
2 teaspoons vinegar (red wine or apple cider)
1/2 a small onion
2 teaspoons paprika
fresh or dried oregano, to taste (optional)
200g (7oz) diced tomatoes (half a tin)

Enchilada sauce
1/2 a 400g (14oz) tin of tomatoes
1/2 a small onion
pinch or two of cayenne pepper
pinch or two of salt
1 teaspoon vinegar (red wine or apple cider)
1 clove garlic, finely chopped

6 sheets of mountain bread, or tortillas
1 quantity servo-style cheesy sauce (page 76)

Method

Preheat the oven to 160-200c (320-390f).

For the beans, mash all the ingredients together until combined.

For the enchilada sauce: Mix all ingredients together, breaking up the chunks of onion.

To assemble as rolled enchiladas, put about 2 heaped tablespoons of the bean mix on each tortilla and roll up. Put in a 20x30cm (7.8 x 11.8 in) lasagne dish. Repeat for other 5 breads, and put a layer of enchilada sauce on top.

Bake for about 30 minutes.

In the last 5 minutes of baking, make the cheesy sauce according to the directions on page 76. Pour this over the enchiladas and serve right away.

Alternatively this can be layered as a lasagne, using either flatbread or lasagne sheets.

Gluten-free option: Use gluten-free mountain bread or tortillas.

Bean and Kale Enchiladas

Ingredients
2-3 cups finely chopped kale or other leafy green
1 small onion (preferably red), diced
400g (14oz) diced tomatoes
3-5 cloves of garlic
1 teaspoon ground cumin
2 teaspoons dried oregano
1/4 -1 teaspoon cayenne pepper
1/2-1 teaspoon salt
3 teaspoons vinegar (red wine or apple cider)
1 1/2 cups cooked 4 bean mix (1 400g (14oz) tin)
6 sheets mountain bread or tortillas
1 1/2 cups cooked red kidney beans (1 400g (14oz) tin)

Method
Preheat oven to 160-200c (320-390f).

Chop the kale using a food processor, and place in a mixing bowl.

Put half the onion in a food processor, and the other half in the mixing bowl with the kale.

Add the tin of tomatoes, garlic herbs, spices and vinegar to the food processor and blend until combined. Add half of this mixture (3/4 cup) to the mixing bowl, and leave the rest in the food processor.

Add the 4 bean mix to the mixing bowl, and mix until combined.

Put about 5 tablespoons of this mixture in each sheet of bread, roll up, and place in a 20x30cm (7.8 x 11.8 in) lasagne dish.

Add the kidney beans to the tomatoes in the food processor, blend until smooth and adjust seasonings to taste. Pour this over the rolled enchiladas and bake for 30 minutes.

78   **Gluten-free option:** Use gluten-free mountain bread or tortillas.

Quiche

Ingredients

LF NF option

For the crust:

1 1/2 cups flour (wholemeal wheat, spelt, barley or gluten-free)
1/4 teaspoon salt
1/4 cup tahini or oil
water, as needed (at least 1/4 cup)

Makes 2 big serves, or
up to 8 smaller serves

For the filling:

1 cup chickpea flour (besan)
1 1/2 teaspoons salt
1 1/2 teaspoons cracked pepper
1 tablespoon dijon mustard (optional)
1 1/2 cups water
a handful of fresh chives or a small onion, very finely chopped
optional handful each of fresh parsley and celery leaves, finely chopped
1 dinner plate of finely chopped fast cooking vegetables (e.g.: broccoli, cauliflower, kale, cabbage, green beans, zucchini, capsicum, tomato), or precooked slower-cooking vegetables (potato, sweet potato, pumpkin)
1 small carrot, diced
1 small onion, cut into half moons
optional 1 tomato, sliced

Method

Preheat the oven to 160-200c (320-390f).

In a mixing bowl, evenly blend the tahini with the flour and salt, until crumbly. Add the water a little at a time, mixing with a fork or your hands, until it presses together without being too dry.

Press this into a greased 20cm (8") springform pan, prick the bottom with a fork a few times and bake for 10 minutes.

Prepare the filling by mixing the chickpea flour, salt and pepper, breaking up any lumps with a fork. Slowly add the mustard and water, making sure that no lumps form. Chop all the veggies on the dinner plate and add them to the mix, along with the carrot and herbs. Place in the prebaked crust, top with the onion half-moons and sliced tomato and bake for around 45-75 minutes, until golden and firm.

Nightshade-free option: Be sure not to include any tomatoes, capsicums, chilies, eggplants or potatoes.
Gluten-free option: Use a gluten-free flour blend in the crust.

SIDE DISHES

Paratha

A wholemeal Indian flatbread

Ingredients

1 cup wholemeal wheat flour
pinch of salt
1/2 cup water, plus extra, if needed
1 tablespoon oil

Extra flour and oil, for rolling and brushing

Method

Mix the flour and salt together, then add the water and oil. Knead for 1 minute. Leave to rest for 10 minutes, covered.

Place a little flour on a plate.

Divide the dough into four balls, then roll in hands until smooth. Roll in the flour.

Roll each piece of dough out into a 10cm (4") circle. Brush with some oil, then fold in half to form a semicircle. Brush with oil again, then fold in half again to form a triangle. Roll or stretch each one out as big as you think as you can get it without breaking.

Heat a frying pan to high heat, cook the parathas one by one, brushing with extra oil if you wish.

Baked Pakoras

A delicious and healthy curry accompaniment or entrée that can be made while the curry is simmering on the stove.

Ingredients

2 cups chickpea flour (besan)
2 teaspoons coriander, ground
1/4 - 1 teaspoon cayenne pepper
2 teaspoons salt
3/4 cup water
1 tablespoon apple cider vinegar or lemon juice
3 cups diced or finely chopped quick-cooking vegetables (cauliflower and cabbage are both delicious, so is a little onion)
4 big leaves kale or silverbeet, ripped into small pieces.

Kitchen time 5-10 minutes
Baking time 15-25 minutes

LF NF option OGF
option
(under 45 minutes)

Makes 4 serves

Method

Preheat the oven to 175-250c (375-500f).

Mix the dry ingredients with a fork, breaking up any lumps. Slowly add the water and vinegar. Mix in the vegetables, then the kale.

Brush a baking tray with oil and place heaped tablespoons of the mixture on it. Bake for 15-25 minutes, until firm and golden. Flip over 3/4 of the way through, brushing with oil if you wish.

Nighshade-free option: Omit the cayenne pepper

Hash Browns

Ingredients

400g (14oz) potatoes (3 or 4 medium sized ones)
1/4 cup chickpea flour
1/2 teaspoon salt
3-4 tablespoons vegan milk

Method

Grate the potatoes and place in a tea towel. Squeeze out as much liquid as you can, then combine in a mixing bowl with the chickpea flour and salt. Stir through the vegan milk.

Heat 2-3 tablespoons of oil in a frying pan over medium high heat. When it sizzles when flicked with water, add heaped tablespoons of the potato mixture, making sure they are no higher than 1cm (1/3"). Cook for a few minutes on one side until golden, then flip over and cook until the other side is golden. Serve right away.

Low fat option: Follow the instructions on page 39 for oven-baked hash browns.
Nightshade-free option: Use sweet potatoes or swede (rutabaga) instead of the potatoes.

Kartoffelpuffer

Ingredients

4 medium potatoes - 400-450g (14-16 oz)
1 small onion
1/4 cup chickpea flour
1/2 teaspoon salt
3-4 tablespoons vegan milk
optional 2 tablespoons nutritional yeast (savoury yeast flakes)
optional 1 tablespoon hot mustard
optional 1/2 teaspoon cracked pepper

Method

Grate the potatoes and onion and place in a tea towel. Squeeze out as much liquid as you can, then place in a mixing bowl with the chickpea flour and salt. Add the vegan milk, a little at a time, along with any other ingredients you're using.

Heat 2-3 tablespoons of oil in a frying pan over medium high heat. When it sizzles when flicked with water, add heaped tablespoons of the potato mixture, making sure they are no higher than 1 1/2 cm (2/3"). Cook for a few minutes on one side, until golden, then flip over and cook until the other side is golden. Serve right away.

These are really nice served with cashew sour cream (page 60)

82

Nightshade-free option: Use swede (rutabaga) instead of the potatoes.

Oven Chips

Kitchen time 5-10 minutes
Baking time 20-40 minutes

NSI **LF NF option**
OGF (under 45 minutes)

Serves 2

Ingredients
400-500g (14-18oz) potatoes or sweet potatoes
2 teaspoons oil
4-7 pinches of salt

Method
Preheat the oven to 160-200c (320-390f).

Peel the sweet potatoes, if using.

Cut the potatoes or sweet potatoes into slices as thick or thin as you would like, then slice into chip shapes.

Place on a baking sheet with the oil, and flip them around in it, making sure they're all coated. Move them around so that none are touching, then sprinkle with the salt.

Bake for 20-40 minutes, depending on the size of your chips. It's a good idea to flip them all over after 10-15 minutes, or to shake the tray, to make sure that one side isn't getting overcooked.

Thicker chips work best with this, because thin chips tend to get overcooked very quickly.

Variation: For spicy chips, you can sprinkle these with 2 or more pinches of cayenne pepper, and a few pinches of paprika before baking.

Fast Roasted Vegetables

Kitchen time 5-10 minutes
Baking time 10-20 minutes

NSI **LF NF option**
OGF (under 45 minutes)

Serves 2

Ingredients
Water, for boiling
400-500g (14-18oz) potatoes, sweet potatoes or pumpkin
2 teaspoons oil
4-7 pinches of salt
optional florets of cauliflower or slices of zucchini

Method
Preheat the oven to 160-200c (320-390f).

Bring a pot of water to the boil.

Chop the vegetables into small pieces (the smaller they are, the crispier they will get in the oven)

Boil them until tender, around 15-20 minutes. Drain.

Place the vegetables on a baking sheet with the oil, and flip them around in it, making sure they're all coated. Sprinkle with salt. You can add some cauliflower or zucchini now if you like.

Bake for 10-20 minutes, until they're as crispy as you'd like them to be.

Balsamic Seared Broccoli

Kitchen time 5-10 minutes

NSI **LF NF** OGF
(under 45 minutes)

Serves 2

Ingredients

1 head of broccoli
1-2 teaspoons oil
2 pinches of salt
1-2 teaspoons balsamic vinegar

Method

Cut the broccoli into smaller florets, making sure they're all around the same size by cutting the bigger ones up more.

Heat the oil over medium-high heat in a frying pan. When it's hot, add the broccoli and stir-fry to coat it all in the oil. Spread it out into one layer and sprinkle with the salt. Let it sit for 30-60 seconds, until slightly charred in places, then continue to stir-fry for a couple more minutes until the colour changes to a vibrant green. Take off the heat and quickly add the balsamic vinegar, stirring to coat. Serve right away.

Crispy Kale Chips

Kitchen time 5 minutes
Baking time 8-11 minutes

NSI **LF NF** OGF
(under 45 minutes)

Serves 2

Ingredients

4 big leaves of curly kale, or about 10 leaves of bumpy tuscan (dinosaur) kale
1 teaspoon olive oil
a pinch of salt

Method

Preheat the oven to 160-200c (320-390f).

Rip the kale into small, even pieces. Put the oil and salt in a bowl, then add all the kale, rubbing it in to make sure it's all evenly coated.

Place on a baking tray in a single layer and bake for 8-11 minutes, until crispy but not overcooked. They go from uncooked to overcooked very quickly, so make sure to keep checking them regularly after 8 minutes.

Spätzle

To make these Swabian noodles to serve with any of the seitan dishes, make the mixture while the seitan is baking. When the seitan is finished, switch off the oven and boil the spätzle.

LF NF OGF
(under 45 minutes)

Serves 2

Ingredients

1 cup wholemeal wheat flour
1/2 cup chickpea flour (besan)
1/8-1/4 teaspoon ground nutmeg
1/4 teaspoon ground black pepper
1/2 teaspoon salt
3/4 cup vegan milk

Method

Mix the dry ingredients together, breaking up any lumps. Slowly add the vegan milk and mix for 2-3 minutes. Leave to sit for at least 15 minutes.

Bring a large pot of water to the boil.

Because the spätzle cook really quickly, be sure to cook them after the rest of the meal is finished, including any salads.

To form the noodles, take small pieces of the dough with your hands and stretch them out as long as they will get. Drop into the boiling water and repeat for the rest of the dough, working quickly and not being too finicky about the shapes.

When all the noodles have risen to the top, drain them.

For best results sauté the cooked noodles in some oil, maybe with some onion or fresh herbs. Serve straight away.

Gluten-free option: Use a gluten-free flour blend in place of the wheat flour.

Austrian Jam Biscuits

Ingredients

1/4 cup chickpea flour (besan) or flaxseed meal
1/2 cup raw sugar or rapadura
1/4 cup water (boiling if using flaxseed)
1/2 cup coconut oil, melted
1 teaspoon vanilla extract
1 1/4 cups flour (barley, wholemeal spelt, wholewheat pastry or gluten-free)

2/3 cup ground almonds, or almond meal, optional
1/2 cup jam of your choice

NF OGF
(under 45 minutes)

Makes 15

Method

Preheat the oven to 130-170c (265-340f).

In a mixing bowl, combine the chickpea flour and sugar, breaking up any lumps. Add the water, coconut oil and vanilla and stir until well combined. Stir in the barley flour to create a sticky dough.

Take heaped teaspoons of the mixture, and roll into balls. Roll each one in the almonds, then flatten to about 1cm (1/2") thick.

Place on a greased or lined baking tray, and using your thumb or a teaspoon, make a dent in each biscuit for the jam to go in.

Put a little jam in each biscuit and bake for 15-20 minutes.

Peanut Butter Biscuits

These biscuits are chewy and crunchy with delicious peanut butter and caramel flavours. They are great on their own, or drizzled with melted vegan chocolate.

Ingredients

3/4 cup to 1 cup raw sugar or rapadura
1/4 cup chickpea flour (besan)
3/4 cup peanut butter
1/4 cup oil (olive, melted coconut or sunflower)
1/4 cup water
1 teaspoon vanilla extract
1 teaspoon barley malt syrup
1 1/2 cups flour (barley, wholemeal spelt, wholewheat pastry or gluten-free)
1 teaspoon baking powder

Method

Preheat the oven to 160-200c (320-390f).

In a mixing bowl, combine the sugar and chickpea flour, breaking up any lumps.

In a separate bowl or measuring cup, mix the peanut butter, oil, water, vanilla and barley malt until combined. Add this to the sugar and chickpea flour, stirring well to combine.

Stir through the flour and baking powder. Take heaped teaspoons of the mixture and roll into balls, place on a greased or lined baking tray and flatten with a wet fork. Bake for 12-15 minutes, until the bottoms are lightly browned.

Danish Chocolate Orange Biscuits

Kitchen time 15 minutess
Baking time 10-15 minutes

Ingredients

NF OGF
(under 45 minutes)

Makes 20

1/4 cup raw sugar or rapadura
1/4 cup chickpea flour (besan)
3 tablespoons finely grated orange peel
1/4 cup orange juice or water
1/2 cup coconut oil, melted
1 1/2 cups flour (barley, wholemeal spelt, wholewheat pastry or gluten-free)
100g (3.5oz) melted chocolate, for dipping

Method

Preheat the oven to 160-200c (320-390f).

In a mixing bowl, combine the sugar, chickpea flour and orange peel. Stir though the orange juice and the coconut oil, then mix in the flour.

Take heaped teaspoons of the mixture and roll into balls. Place on a greased or lined baking tray and flatten with a wet fork. Bake for 10-15 minutes, until lightly browned on the bottom. Alternatively, the mixture can be refrigerated for 20 minutes, then rolled out and cut into shapes.

Melt the chocolate by bringing a saucepan to the boil with a tiny bit of water in it. Place a metal or glass mixing bowl over this, making sure it is not touching the water. Turn the heat down to the lowest possible setting and add the chocolate.

Dip one half of each biscuit in the melted chocolate, then leave to cool.
Alternatively, drizzle the chocolate over the top of the biscuits.

Oat and Cinnamon Biscuits

A healthy and delicious biscuit. Flaxseed meal and boiling water works really well in this, in place of the chickpea flour and water (see replacing eggs, page 7).

Ingredients
3/4 cup rolled oats
3/4 cup flour (barley, wholemeal spelt or wholewheat pastry)
1/4 cup chickpea flour (besan)
1/3 cup raw sugar or rapadura
a pinch of salt
3/4 teaspoon cinnamon
1/2 teaspoon bicarb soda
1/3 cup sultanas (raisins) or vegan chocolate chips, optional
1/4 cup grated apple (1 very small one) or apple sauce
1/4 cup water
2 tablespoons oil (melted coconut, olive or sunflower)
1 teaspoon vanilla extract
1 teaspoon barley malt syrup (optional)

Method
Preheat the oven to 160-200c (320-390f).

90

In a mixing bowl, combine the dry ingredients. Add the wet ingredients and stir until evenly mixed. Place heaped teaspoons of the mixture on a greased or lined baking tray, flatten with a wet fork, and bake for 8-12 minutes, until the bottoms are brown.

Golden Biscuits

Kitchen time 10 minutes
Baking time 10 minutes

NSI **LF NF** OGF
(under 45 minutes)

Makes 30

These are crunchy on the outside and chewy on the inside with a delicious caramel and vanilla taste.

Ingredients

2 cups flour (barley, wholemeal spelt, wholewheat pastry or gluten-free)
3/4 cup raw sugar or rapadura
1 teaspoon baking powder
a pinch of salt
1/4 cup water
1/2 cup oil (melted coconut, olive or sunflower)
1 tablespoon barley malt syrup, golden syrup or molasses*
2 teaspoons vanilla extract
Optional 2 handfuls walnuts, finely chopped

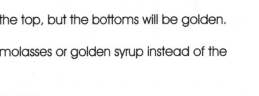

Method

Preheat the oven to 160-200c (320-390f).

Grease or line 2 baking sheets.

In a mixing bowl, combine the dry ingredients until evenly mixed. In a separate bowl or measuring cup, combine the wet ingredients. Add the wet ingredients to the dry, stirring to incorporate all the flour, and create a sticky dough.

Place heaped teaspoons of the mixture onto the baking sheets, flatten with a wet fork and, put in the oven and bake for around 10 minutes. If you're baking this on 2 oven shelves, switch them over about halfway through the baking, so that both trays bake evenly.

When these are ready, they will appear soft and slightly undercooked on the top, but the bottoms will be golden.

Gluten-free option: Use a gluten-free flour blend for the flour, and use molasses or golden syrup instead of the barley malt.

*If you don't have any of these, you could use brown sugar in place of the sugar

Chocolate Biscuits

Kitchen time 10 minutes
Baking time 10 minutes

NSI **LF NF** OGF
(under 45 minutes)

Makes 30

Ingredients

1/2 cup cocoa
2 cups flour (barley, wholemeal spelt, wholewheat pastry or gluten-free)
1 cup raw sugar or rapadura
1 teaspoon baking powder
a pinch of salt
1/3 cup water
1/2 cup oil (melted coconut, olive or sunflower)
1/2 teaspoon vanilla extract
1-3 teaspoons barley malt syrup, golden syrup or molasses
Optional 2 handfuls walnuts, finely chopped

Method

Same as for Golden Biscuits, above.

Lemon Slice

A shortcrust base with a soft lemon topping.

Ingredients

For the base:
1/2 cup coconut oil, melted
1/4 cup raw sugar or rapadura
1 teaspoon lemon zest
a pinch of salt
1 cup flour (barley, wholemeal spelt, wholewheat pastry or gluten-free)

For the topping (make this while the base is baking):
1/2-3/4 cup raw sugar or rapadura
1/2 cup chickpea flour (besan)
2 tablespoons flour (barley, wholemeal spelt, wholewheat pastry or gluten-free)
1 tablespoon lemon zest
1/2 teaspoon baking powder
1/2 cup water
1/3 cup lemon juice

Method

Preheat the oven to 160-200c (320-390f).

To make the base, mix the coconut oil, sugar, lemon zest and salt together, then add the barley flour to form a crumbly shortcrust. Press into a greased or lined 20cm (8") or 20 x 30cm (8x12") lasagne dish and bake for 15 minutes.

While the base is baking, mix the dry ingredients of the topping together, breaking up any lumps. Slowly add the wet ingredients, a little at the time, stirring in between each addition to make sure there are no lumps. Pour on top of the base once it has been in the oven for 15 minutes, and bake for around 20 minutes, until set in the middle with golden edges.

The cooking times for this are given for a glass or ceramic baking dish, if you're using a metal one, be sure to check to see if it's ready 5 minutes earlier than the times I have given.

Chocolate Brownie Slice

While this recipe is healthier and easier to make than most of the brownie recipes out there, it tastes every bit as good.

Ingredients

1 1/4 - 1 1/2 cups raw sugar or rapadura
2 cups flour (barley, wholemeal spelt, wholewheat pastry or gluten-free)
2 tablespoons chickpea flour (besan)
2/3 cup cocoa
1 teaspoon baking powder
a pinch of salt

1/2 cup coconut oil (melted) or fruit purée
2/3 cup water
1 teaspoon vanilla extract

Optional nuts or vegan chocolate chips for topping (walnuts are really nice)

Method

Preheat the oven to 130-170c (265-340f). Grease and flour a 20 x 30cm (8x12") lasagne dish.

Mix the dry ingredients together until evenly combined. Thoroughly mix in the wet ingredients until there is no trace left of the dry ingredients (the batter will be very thick). Put in the lasagne dish and bake for 20-25 minutes for a glass dish, less if you're using a metal tin.

It may not look quite done at the end of this time, but it will finish cooking outside the oven. It's better to have it slightly undercooked than overcooked.

Fruit Muffins

A really simple and tasty recipe that works with most fruits, or vegan chocolate chips.

NSI **LF option NF**
OGF (under 45 minutes)

Ingredients

1 1/2 cups flour (barley, wholemeal spelt, wholewheat pastry or gluten-free)
2 teaspoons baking powder
1/2 cup raw sugar or rapadura
pinch of salt
optional 1 teaspoon cinnamon
3/4 cup vegan milk
1/4 cup oil (melted coconut, olive or sunflower) or apple purée
optional 1 teaspoon vanilla extract
2/3 cup finely chopped fruit, or whole berries (e.g. apple, pear, strawberry, blueberry, raspberry, red currant etc)

Makes 6

Optional crumbly topping:

2 tablespoons sugar
2 tablespoons flour
1/2 teaspoon cinnamon
1 tablespoon oil (olive, melted coconut or sunflower)

Method

Preheat the oven to 160-200c (320-390f).

If you're using the crumbly topping, make this first by mixing the dry ingredients together in a small bowl, and then stirring through the oil, crumbling it with your fingers until it's all evenly mixed.

To make the muffins, combine the dry ingredients in a mixing bowl, then add the vegan milk, oil and vanilla and stir until no traces of flour remain. Fold in the fruit, then spoon into a muffin tin. Top with the crumbly topping if using, and bake for 15-20 minutes.

Chocolate Self-Saucing Pudding

Kitchen time 5-10 minutes
Baking time 45 minutes

NSI
LF option NF OGF

Serves 2-4

This delicious dessert is quick to make and can be mixed and baked in the same dish. While baking, the topping turns into a thick chocolate sauce and magically moves from the top of the pudding to the bottom, with a rich chocolate cake layer on the top.

Ingredients

1 cup flour (barley, wholemeal spelt, wholewheat pastry or gluten-free)
2 teaspoons baking powder
1/2 cup raw sugar or rapadura
2 tablespoons cocoa powder
1/2 cup water
2 tablespoons oil or apple purée
1 teaspoon vanilla extract

For the topping:
2/3 cup raw sugar or rapadura
1/4 cup cocoa
1 3/4 cups hot water

Method

Preheat the oven to 160-200c (320-390f).

In a 8" circle casserole dish or lasagne pan combine the flour, baking powder, sugar and cocoa powder. Add the water, oil and vanilla. Stir until no traces of flour remain. Flatten the mixture, so that it's at an even height, then sprinkle with 2/3 cup sugar and 1/4 cup cocoa.

Pour the hot water over the top of it and bake for 45 minutes, until the cake layer is on the top and looks baked.

Variation: Chocolate and Orange Self-Saucing Pudding

Zest and juice 2 oranges. Use 1/2 cup orange juice in place of the water in the cake layer, and add all the zest to this.

Add extra water to the remaining orange juice to make it 1 3/4 cups in volume. Bring this to the boil and use this in place of the hot water for pouring over the top.

Chocolate Zucchini Mud Cake

Don't be fooled by the zucchini in the title, this is actually a decadent tasting mud cake. Made in a bundt pan it is thin and crispy on the outside, and moist and dense on the inside, so much that it doesn't need any icing or accompaniments, but to make it a bit fancier-looking you could drizzle it with melted vegan chocolate or icing. This mixture also makes delicious muffins, making 24 medium sized ones.

Kitchen time 10-15 minutes
Baking time 60 minutes

LF option
NF OGF
(under 45 minutes option)

Ingredients
2 cups flour (barley, wholemeal spelt, wholewheat pastry or gluten-free)
1 3/4 cups raw sugar or rapadura
3/4 cup cocoa
3/4 cup chickpea flour (besan)
1 teaspoon bicarb soda
1/2 teaspoon baking powder
a pinch of salt
3/4 cup oil or apple purée
3/4 cup water
1 1/2 - 2 cups grated zucchini
2 teaspoons vanilla extract

Method
Preheat the oven to 160-200c (320-390f).

Grease and flour a large bundt pan, or some muffin tins.

In a mixing bowl, combine the flour, sugar, cocoa, chickpea flour, bicarb soda, baking powder and salt. Break up any lumps and mix until evenly combined.

In a separate mixing bowl, combine the oil, water, zucchini and vanilla. Add this to the dry ingredients, stirring until no traces of flour remain.

Pour into the bundt tin and bake for around an hour, until the top is firm and the knife comes out with a couple of moist crumbs (not batter!) when put through the middle of it. Leave to cool for 10 minutes, then run a knife around the outside and invert onto a plate. Leave the bundt tin on top while it cools. Best served after it has cooled down.

Under 45 minute option: Bake as 24 muffins for 20-25 minutes.

Apple and Cinnamon Bundt Cake

Kitchen time 10-15 minutes
Baking time 45-70 minutes

LF option
NF OGF

Ingredients

3 1/2 cups flour (barley, wholemeal spelt, wholewheat pastry or gluten-free)
3/4 cup chickpea flour (besan)
1 cup raw sugar or rapadura
2 1/2 teaspoons baking powder
3 teaspoons cinnamon
a pinch of salt
2/3 cup oil (melted coconut, olive or sunflower) or apple purée
2 teaspoons vanilla extract
1/4 cup lemon juice or apple cider vinegar
1 3/4 cups water
3 cups finely chopped or sliced apples (around 4 small ones)

Method

Preheat the oven to 160-200c (320-390f). Grease and flour a large bundt pan.

Mix the dry ingredients together, breaking up any lumps. Fold through the wet ingredients until no traces of flour remain, and then gently fold in the apples. Pour into the pan and gently bang to remove any air bubbles. Bake for 45-70 minutes.

Chocolate Caramel and Almond Torte

The most decadent of all my recipes, perfect for a special occasion.

Kitchen time 20 minutes
Baking time 15-30 minutes
Setting time 1-2 hours

Ingredients

1 cup almonds (or almond meal, if you don't have a food processor)
1 cup rolled oats (or extra flour, if you don't have a food processor)
2/3 cup flour (barley, wholemeal spelt, wholewheat pastry or gluten-free)
1/3 cup raw sugar or rapadura
a pinch of salt
1 teaspoon vanilla extract
1/4 cup water, plus extra if needed.

GF option **NF** OGF

For the caramel layer:
1/3 cup coconut oil, melted
1 cup raw sugar or rapadura
2-3 teaspoons barley malt syrup, golden syrup or molasses
1/2 cup vegan milk
a pinch of salt

1 cup roasted almonds*, finely chopped

For the chocolate layer:
1/3 cup coconut oil, melted
250g (8.8oz) dark vegan chocolate
2/3 cup vegan milk

*To roast the almonds, see bottom of page 113

Method

First make the base by preheating the oven to 160-200c (320-390f). Combine the almonds, oats, salt, sugar and flour in a food processor. Blend until fine. If you don't have a food processor, use almond meal and extra flour in place of the oats. Add the vanilla and water, mixing well. Add any extra water as needed until it starts to stick together well.

Press into a 23cm (9") or 20cm (8") springform pan and bake for 15-30 minutes, until golden. Refrigerate or freeze this while you make the caramel layer. If any cracks appear, brush with a little coconut oil to prevent the caramel layer from soaking through.

To make the caramel sauce, put all the ingredients in a saucepan over medium-low heat and bring to the boil, stirring constantly. Keep boiling it while stirring for another 2 minutes, making sure that all the sugar is dissolved. When it is ready, pour it into the baked crust and top with 2/3 of the chopped toasted almonds. Leave to cool.

This caramel sauce is runnier than the one in the photo. If you'd like a more solid caramel layer, use 1/2 a cup of coconut oil instead of 1/3 cup, and reduce the vegan milk to 1/3 cup.

To make the chocolate layer, bring a saucepan with a tiny bit of water in it to the boil. Place a metal or glass mixing bowl over this, making sure it is not touching the water. Turn the heat down to the lowest possible setting and add the coconut oil and chocolate. Be patient and wait for it to completely melt, then gently stir through the vegan milk. Pour this on top of the caramel layer, and top with the rest of the roasted almonds to decorate. Put in the fridge for at least 2 hours, or the freezer for at least 1 hour to set.

This makes 12-16 serves and keeps well at room temperature for a week. It also freezes very well.

Gluten-free option: Use a gluten-free flour blend instead of the barley flour and oats. Use golden syrup or molasses in the caramel layer, and make sure your vegan milk is gluten-free.

Chocolate Cakes and Chocolate Icing

Kitchen time 5-10 minutes
Baking time 35-70 minutes

GF option NSI
LF option NF OGF
(under 45 minutes option)

I have included two chocolate cake recipes here, to fit different sized cake tins. Both can be made from ingredients found in most non-vegan kitchens, are easy to make, and are very chocolaty and delicious.

To fit a 23cm (9") round cake tin

Ingredients

2 2/3 cups flour (barley, wholemeal spelt, wholewheat pastry or gluten-free)
1/2 cup cocoa
1 cup raw sugar or rapadura
2 teaspoons bicarb soda
a pinch of salt
2 cups water
2/3 cup oil (melted coconut, olive or sunflower) or apple purée
2 tablespoons vinegar, preferably balsamic
1 teaspoon vanilla extract
optional teaspoon barley malt syrup (or molasses for gluten-free)

Method

Preheat the oven to 160-200c (320-390f). Grease and flour a cake tin.

In a mixing bowl, combine the dry ingredients, breaking up any lumps and stirring until evenly mixed.

Once the oven has finished heating up, add the wet ingredients and stir through until no traces of flour remain.

Pour into the cake tin and bake for 45-70 minutes, until a knife poked into the centre comes out clean.

To fit a 20cm (8") round cake tin, or a small loaf tin (under 45 minutes)

Ingredients

1 1/2 cups flour (barley, wholemeal spelt, wholewheat pastry or gluten-free)
1/4 cup cocoa
3/4 cup raw sugar or rapadura
1 teaspoon bicarb soda
a pinch of salt
1 cup water
1/3 cup oil (melted coconut, olive or sunflower) or apple purée
1 tablespoon vinegar
1 teaspoon vanilla extract
optional teaspoon barley malt syrup (or molasses for gluten-free)

Method

Follow the instructions for the 23cm (9") cake,
but bake for 35-45 minutes instead.

Chocolate Icing

Ingredients

1/3 cup cocoa
1/2 cup raw sugar or rapadura
1/3 cup vegan milk
1/3-1/2 cup coconut oil
1 teaspoon vanilla extract

Method

In a small saucepan, combine all the ingredients and bring to the boil. Reduce the heat and simmer for a minute, until all the sugar is melted, stirring constantly. Take off the heat and continue to stir every now and then. It will thicken as it cools.

Black Forest Cake

The Black Forest cake is named after the Black Forest cherry liquor that is traditionally sprinkled over both layers of the cake before the ganache and cream is added, so if you have anything like this in the cupboard, you might like to use it. I have never made it this way, and think it is just as special without it.

Ingredients
1 recipe chocolate cake (page 100), for either size round cake tin, baked and cooled
optional 1 recipe chocolate icing (page 100)
at least 400g (14oz) fresh dark cherries, pitted and halved (you can use frozen or canned ones if you really want)
grated chocolate, for sprinkling over the top

Almond cream:
1 1/2 cups blanched almonds (to blanch, add to boiling water and boil for a minute or two, until the skins can be slipped off. Drain and run cold water over them, slipping all the skins off.)
1/4 cup maple syrup or sugar
1 1/4 - 1 1/2 cups water

Method
To make the almond cream:
If using sugar, bring 1/4 cup of water to the boil with the sugar, while stirring. Simmer until dissolved.

In a blender or food processor, combine the blanched almonds and half the water. Blend until smooth, adding a little more water as you need to. Add the syrup, along with extra water to blend it to a thick, creamy consistency. If there are chunks of almonds that don't seem to be getting blended, you could strain it through a mesh strainer, to get the smoothest possible cream. It's not the end of the world if there are a few small chunks left, they will soften a little more as the cake is refrigerated.

To assemble the cake:
First carefully slice the cake through the middle with a bread knife, to make two thinner circles. The best way to do this is with the cake flat on the serving dish, cutting it very slowly. If you are not feeling that confident in this, you could first halve or quarter the cake and then slice it. Take the top layer off and put it aside for the moment.

On the bottom layer of the cake, spread half the chocolate icing, if using. Top with 1/3 of the almond cream, along with a layer of cherries. Put the top layer of the cake on top of this.

Spread the rest of the chocolate icing over the top layer. Place the remaining almond cream on the top, spreading or drizzling some along the sides of the cake as well. Top with another layer of cherries, then sprinkle with grated chocolate. Place in the fridge for as long as you have the patience. Tastes best after it's been in the fridge for a day or two, but still very tasty served right away.

Chocolate Hazelnut Cake

A delicious variation on plain chocolate cake with a rich hazelnut icing that tastes like an organic vegan version of chocolate hazelnut spread, but much nicer. It's really nice with a layer of hazelnut cream in the middle, but also very tasty as a single layer cake iced with the chocolate hazelnut icing.

Kitchen time 10-15 minutes
Baking time 35-70 minutes

NF OGF
(under 45 minutes option)

Ingredients

1 recipe chocolate cake (page 100), for either size cake tin, baked and cooled.

Optional hazelnut cream
3/4 cup hazelnuts, roasted*
1/2 cup water
1-2 tablespoons maple syrup, or sugar dissolved in boiling water

Chocolate hazelnut icing
3/4 cup hazelnuts, roasted*
1/3 cup coconut oil
1/2 cup vegan milk
1/3 cup cocoa
1/2 cup raw sugar or rapadura

Method
To make the hazelnut cream:
Take as many of the skins off the hazelnuts as possible and place in a blender or food processor with half the water. Continue to add more water as needed, to create a thick and smooth cream. Add the rest of the water along with the syrup.

To make the chocolate hazelnut icing: In a food processor, grind the hazelnuts until fine, either in small even chunks or add the sugar and grind into a very fine meal.

Place the ground hazelnuts, and the rest of the ingredients in a small saucepan and bring to the boil, stirring constantly. Reduce heat and simmer while stirring until the sugar dissolves. Take off the heat and stir every now and then. It will thicken as it cools.

To assemble the cake as 2 layers: Follow the slicing directions on page 101 to slice through the middle. Place all the hazelnut cream on top of the bottom layer, top with the other layer and spread the chocolate hazelnut icing over the top, drizzling some down the sides if you wish.

For better presentation, use a few extra roasted hazelnuts to decorate the top of the cake, either whole or roughly chopped.

*To roast the hazelnuts, preheat the oven to 160-200c (320-390f). Place the hazelnuts in a single layer in a glass or ceramic baking dish and bake for 15-20 minutes, until they taste roasted. This will take less time if you use a metal baking dish, so be sure to check after 10 minutes.

Marble Cake

Ingredients

1 cup raw sugar or rapadura
1/2 cup chickpea flour (besan)
2 1/2 cups flour (barley, wholemeal spelt, wholewheat pastry or gluten-free)
2 1/2 teaspoons baking powder
a pinch of salt
2/3 cup oil or apple purée
2 teaspoons vanilla extract
1 1/2 cups vegan milk

LF option NF OGF

For the chocolate marble:
3 tablespoons cocoa
2 tablespoons sugar
2 tablespoons vegan milk

Method

Preheat the oven to 160-200c (320-390f). Grease and flour a large bundt pan.

In a mixing bowl, combine the sugar, chickpea flour, barley flour, baking powder and salt, breaking up any lumps.

Add the oil, vanilla and vegan milk, stirring until no traces of flour remain.

Put half the mixture in a separate bowl, and add the cocoa, sugar and vegan milk, stirring until evenly mixed.

Place a small layer of the vanilla cake mixture in the bundt tin. Top with half the chocolate mixture and gently swirl with a fork, to create a marble effect. Add another layer of vanilla, reserving a few more tablespoons of it, and put the rest of the chocolate mixture on top of this. Top with the rest of the vanilla mixture and gently swirl these top layers with a fork, going around in little circles to create a marble effect.

Bake for 40-50 minutes, until a knife inserted in the centre comes out clean. Drizzle with chocolate icing (page 100) or melted vegan chocolate.

Zucchini Spice Cake

Ingredients

2 cups grated zucchini or carrot
1 1/2 cups raw sugar or rapadura
1 cup sultanas (raisins), or other small or finely chopped dried fruit
1 1/2 teaspoons vanilla extract
1 3/4 cups water
optional 2 teaspoons barley malt syrup (use molasses or golden syrup, for gluten-free option)

NSI **LF NF** OGF

3 cups flour (barley, wholemeal spelt, wholemeal wheat or gluten-free)
3 teaspoons baking powder
1/2 cup finely chopped walnuts, or other nuts
1/2 cup shredded or desiccated coconut
a pinch of salt
optional 1/4 teaspoon ground cardamon or ginger
1 1/2 teaspoons cinnamon
1/2 teaspoon nutmeg
1/4 teaspoon ground cloves

Method

In a medium saucepan combine the zucchini, sugar, sultanas, vanilla and water. Bring to the boil, reduce heat and simmer for 5 minutes. Remove from heat, cover and leave to sit for at least an hour.

Preheat the oven to 160-200c (320-390f). Grease and flour a large bundt pan.

In a mixing bowl combine the flour, baking powder, walnuts, coconut, salt and spices.

Add the zucchini mixture to this, and stir until no traces of flour remain.

Pour the batter into the pan, and gently bang to remove any air from the base of the pan. Bake for around 50-70 minutes, until a knife inserted into the centre comes out clean.

Leave to cool in the tin for 5 minutes, remove from the tin and then cover with lemon glaze.

Lemon Glaze

1/4 cup sugar
2 tablespoons lemon juice
In a small saucepan, combine the sugar and lemon juice. Bring to the boil, stirring constantly, and simmer until the sugar dissolves, a minute or two.

Poke holes in the top and sides of the cake with a fork and slowly pour the glaze over it.

Sticky Date Cake

Kitchen time 5-10 minutes
Baking time 30-35 minutes

LF NF OGF
(under 45 minutes)

This tastes exactly like sticky date pudding when served hot. You would never guess that it doesn't have any added fat. It also tastes nice once it has cooled.

Ingredients

1 1/4 cups chopped dates
1 1/2 cups water
1 teaspoon vanilla extract
1 1/2 cups flour (barley, wholemeal spelt, wholewheat pastry or gluten free)
1/4 cup chickpea flour (besan)
2/3 cup raw sugar or rapadura
1 teaspoon baking powder
1 teaspoon bicarb soda

Method

Preheat the oven to 160-200c (320-390f).

In a small saucepan, bring the dates and water to the boil. Turn off the heat, add the vanilla extract and leave to stand for at least 5 minutes.

Grease and flour a 20cm (8") round cake tin.

In a mixing bowl, combine the flours, sugar, baking powder and bicarb soda. Mash the dates up a bit in the saucepan, then add to the dry ingredients. Pour into the cake tin, and bake for 30-35 minutes.

Optional Caramel Sauce:

1 cup chopped dates
1 cup vegan milk
2 tablespoons barley malt syrup
1/4 cup sugar or maple syrup, to taste

In a small saucepan, bring the dates and the vegan milk to the boil. Let sit for at least 5 minutes, until the dates are mushy. Add the other ingredients and heat it up while stirring when you're ready to serve it. Spoon on top of individual cake slices if serving hot, or just top the entire cake with it.

Linzer Torte

The smell of roasted nuts and cinnamon give this torte a warming, wintery character. Best made with red currants, if you can find them, but raspberry jam is also a good choice.

NF OGF
(under 45 minutes)

Makes 4-8 serves

Ingredients

1 cup hazelnuts or almonds (or meal), toasted for best results, but raw is fine too
1/3 cup raw sugar or rapadura
1/4 cup chickpea flour (besan)
1/2 - 1 teaspoon lemon zest
1/2 cup coconut oil, melted
1/4 cup water
1 1/3 cups flour (barley, wholemeal spelt, wholewheat pastry or gluten free)
1 teaspoon cinnamon
a pinch of salt

1 1/2 cups fresh or frozen red currants and 2/3 cups sugar, or 3/4 cup redcurrant or raspberry jam

Method

Preheat the oven to 160-200c (320-390f). Line the base of a 20 (8") or 23cm (9") springform pan and grease the sides.

Grind the nuts and sugar in a food processor until finely ground.

Place the chickpea flour in a mixing bowl and break up any lumps. Slowly add the water, coconut oil and lemon zest. Add the flour, cinnamon, salt, nuts and sugar and mix until combined.

Take 2/3 of the dough and press it into the lined pan, covering the bottom and pressing it to be about 1cm (1/2") up the sides.

To make the filling from red currants, wash and pick off any non-berry parts of the red currants. Place in a small saucepan with the sugar and bring to the boil while stirring. Reduce the heat and simmer for a couple of minutes, until the sugar is dissolved.

Place the red currant or raspberry filling on top of the base, and top with the rest of the dough, by either rolling it out and cutting it into decorative shapes, or by dividing it up and rolling it into thin sausages, crossing them over the filling to create a pattern.

Bake for 25-35 minutes, until the pastry looks and smells cooked.

SWEET NON-BAKED AND RAW TREATS

Chocolate Mousse

Ingredients

1/3 cup melted vegan dark chocolate (about 85g/3oz)
1/2 - 2/3 cup coconut cream, preferably refrigerated
2 teaspoons maple syrup or sugar

NSI **NF** OGF

Serves 2

Method

To melt the chocolate: bring a tiny bit of water to the boil in a saucepan. Place a glass or metal bowl over it, making sure the bowl isn't touching the water. Reduce the heat to the lowest setting and place the chocolate in the bowl.

When the chocolate is melted, measure out the coconut cream, then beat this and the maple syrup into the chocolate. With some kinds of coconut cream you may have to keep it on the heat for a little longer, and melt it until it's smooth. When the mousse is smooth, pour it into two glasses or small serving dishes and chill for at least an hour. Serve with extra coconut cream and maple syrup if you wish.

Healthy Chocolate Truffles

Tasty and full of nutrition.

Ingredients

2 1/4 - 2 1/2 cups chopped dates
1/3 cup tahini or peanut butter
1/2 cup barley malt syrup (or 1/4 cup maple syrup for gluten-free)
1/3 cup cocoa
1/3 cup chia seeds or 1/2 cup flaxseed meal
1/3 cup walnuts, or other nuts
1/2 cup hazelnuts or almonds
1/2 cup cashews

coconut, cocoa or ground nuts, for rolling

Method

If the dates you're using have hardened, soak them in some boiling water for 10 minutes, then drain.

Mash the dates with the tahini and barley malt syrup until no chunks remain. Mix in the chia seeds or flaxseed meal.

In a food processor, combine the walnuts, cocoa and hazelnuts. Blend until very fine, then add the cashews. Pulse a couple more times, until the cashews are in small, even chunks. Mix all of this into the date mixture.

For best results, leave this in the fridge for at least half an hour before rolling into balls. To roll into balls, take a heaped teaspoon of the mixture, roll it into a ball, and then roll in the coconut, cocoa or ground nuts.

Raw Black Forest Slice

Ingredients

For the cake:
1 1/2 cups walnuts
1 cup dates, soaked if they're a bit dry
1/3 cup cocoa
1/2 teaspoon vanilla extract
extra dates or agave, to taste

NSI **NF** OGF
(under 45 minutes)

For the cherry layer:
30 cherries
1/2 cup shredded or desiccated coconut

For the cream:
1 cup cashews or almonds
3/4 cup water
agave or maple syrup, and vanilla, to taste

For topping:
12 1/2 cherries, pitted and halved
1 square of raw chocolate, grated, or a sprinkling of extra cocoa

Method

To make the cake layer, grind the walnuts in a food processor until crumbly. Add the rest of the ingredients and blend until smooth. Press into a 20cm (8") square or round dish.

Make the cherry layer by pitting 30 cherries and blending these in the food processor with the coconut. Pour this on top of the cake.

To make the cream, combine the cashews and water in a blender and blend until smooth, add sweetener and vanilla, to taste. For best results, soak the cashews before blending; even a few minutes will help. Pour this on top of the cherry layer.

Decorate with the halved cherries, then sprinkle with the chocolate. Best served after it's been in the fridge for a couple of hours Will keep for up to 5 days.

Raw Apricot Crumble Slice

Ingredients

2 cups almonds or other nuts
1 cup shredded or desiccated coconut
1 cup dried apples, apricots or dates
1/4 cup water
optional 1 teaspoon vanilla extract

9 small apricots (around 430g (15oz))

extra 2 tablespoons shredded coconut, optional

Method

In a food processor, blend the nuts, coconut and dried fruit until crumbly. Add the water and vanilla and blend until evenly mixed and sticking together. Take 2/3 of the mixture and press this into a 20cm (8") square or round dish. Put the other 1/3 of the mixture aside for the top layer.

Wash and pit the apricots and blend these in a food processor until smooth-ish. Pour this over the base layer.

Take the remaining 1/3 of the base mixture and crumble it evenly over the top of the apricots. Sprinkle with extra coconut if using, and serve right away or refrigerate for up to 5 days.

Honeycomb

Ingredients
optional 50-100g (1.7-3.5oz) dark vegan chocolate, for covering
4 tablespoons syrup of your choice (I find that 3 tablespoons of maple syrup and 1 tablespoon of barley malt works really well. Rice malt, agave, golden syrup or glucose syrup will also work.)
1 cup raw sugar or rapadura
2 teaspoons bicarb soda

Method
If you're covering the honeycomb with chocolate, melt the chocolate in a glass or metal bowl over a saucepan of water on the lowest setting, making sure the bowl is not touching the water. Spread half of this over a lined 20x30cm (8"x12") tray, to form a thin layer.

To make the honeycomb, put a bowl of cold water near the stove, put the bicarb soda on a separate plate and break up any lumps until it is a fine powder.

Over a medium heat, bring the sugar and syrup to the boil, constantly stirring. Continue to stir over medium heat for a couple more minutes, until it sets when a small amount is dropped in the water, and is brittle and crunchy, not soft.

Take off the heat and quickly stir through the bicarb soda, it will puff up to around 2 to 3 times the size and start to set. Once it is evenly mixed, immediately spoon it into the tray as a layer on top of the chocolate.

Drizzle with the remaining chocolate, if using, and leave to set (or eat bits of it right away... it's messy but it tastes good).

Gluten-free option:
Use a gluten-free syrup such as golden syrup, maple syrup or agave.
Low fat option: Don't use the chocolate

Almond Brittle

Ingredients
1 cup almonds, roasted* and finely or roughly chopped
3/4 cup raw sugar or rapadura
1- 2 teaspoons barley malt, golden syrup or molasses
2 tablespoons water

Method
Grease a 20 x 30 cm (8"x12") dish.

In a small saucepan over medium heat, bring the sugar, syrup and water to the boil. Reduce the heat and simmer, stirring occasionally, for a few minutes, until it sets when a small amount is dropped into cold water, and the texture is brittle, crunchy and not soft.

Remove from the heat and stir through the almonds. Pour into the greased dish and leave to set, drizzling with some melted chocolate if you wish.

Gluten-free option: Use a gluten-free syrup such as golden syrup or molasses.

*To roast the almonds, preheat the oven to 160-200c (320-390f). Place the almonds in a single layer in a glass or ceramic baking dish and bake for 15-20 minutes, until they taste roasted. This will take less time if you use a metal baking dish, so be sure to check after 10 minutes.

Useful Index

For when you want to use a particular ingredient